PRINT CASEBOOKS 6/1984-85 EDITION
THE BEST IN PACKAGING

1984/85 Edition

PRINT CASEBOOKS 6

The Best in

PACKAGING

Written by
Barbara Allen Guilfoyle
J. Roger Guilfoyle

Published by
RC Publications, Inc.
Bethesda, MD

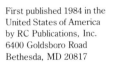

Introduction

**PRINT CASEBOOKS 6/1984-85
EDITION/THE BEST IN
PACKAGING**
Library of Congress Catalog Card
Number 75-649583
ISBN 0-915734-45-1

**PRINT CASEBOOKS 6/1984-85
EDITION**
Complete 6-Volume Set
ISBN 0-915734-40-0

RC PUBLICATIONS
President and Publisher: Howard Cadel
Vice President and Editor: Martin Fox
Art Director/Designer: Andrew P. Kner
Managing Editor: Teresa Reese
Associate Art Director: Glenn Biren
Assistant Editor: Tom Goss
Graphic Production: Linda Riess
Production Assistant: Susan Norr

It is ten years since the first of the Packaging Casebooks was published and 20 since the writers of this book first turned their attention to packaging. In the course of that time, the packaging industry has been buffeted by the changing winds of public concerns. Consumerism and rising costs have altered the political and economic climates, although the dire forecasts that greeted the prospect of "Truth in Packaging" legislation have proved as ephemeral — and as accurate — as the five-day weather forecast.

When we first began writing about packaging design, the conventional thinking was that "Truth in Packaging" would substantively limit design creativity. Those with a vested interest in the prevailing *laissez-faire* atmosphere were full of dark forebodings. In retrospect, most of these fears proved unfounded. As is most often the case, parameters such as those established by "Truth in Packaging" serve to challenge rather than discourage designers.

In the late 1960s, there was also much talk of how the computer was going to affect not only the purchasing habits of housewives but the very manner in which they shopped. Images were projected of the homemaker seated at the computer console in her kitchen. Activating a button, she would call up the daily specials at the supermarket and leisurely shop the information on her screen. Her list completed, the shopper would program her order and charge it to her account with a plastic credit card. The drudgery of marketing would be banished forever, but so would the fun of ferreting out bargains, not to mention impulse-buying.

This scenario proved no more accurate than that for "Truth in Packaging." "Truth in

Packaging" did not reduce the plethora of products available nor did it inhibit design ingenuity. The need to accommodate mandated information and eliminate solecisms could hardly stifle the marketeer's penchant for hyperbole. In the same manner, while the computer dramatically changed marketing procedures, it is at the cash register and not at her kitchen console that the housewife experiences its impact. It is with cash in hand that she watches sophisticated checkout equipment ring up her order today.

As is frequently the case, radical intentions do not ensure revolutionary results. Clearly, when "Truth in Packaging" was proposed, the legislation was designed to protect consumer interests. There can be little question that a certain amount of this has been achieved in the intervening years. However, when one thinks of protecting consumers today, there is less concern about curbing flights of advertising fancy and more anxiety about preventing the illicit adulteration of a package's contents. The Tylenol case has put terrorism on the shelves of the self-service market.

While it may never be known who perpetrated the Tylenol deaths and why, the case is another chilling example of human vulnerability in these anarchistic times. The random violence of skyjackings and urban bombings now lurks in the familiar homeliness of the medicine chest.

Johnson & Johnson's response to the Tylenol tragedy was swift and effective. Even though it can be argued that the company had little choice in the affair, J&J still must be commended for the manner in which it handled a problem it could neither anticipate nor prevent. A steady stream of information issued from the corporate headquarters in New

Brunswick, New Jersey, and company executives appeared frequently on TV and were extensively quoted by the media. Within days of its recall, efforts were underway to reintroduce the product in a package that could be clearly perceived as pilfer-resistant. At the same time, considerable thought was given to the matter of the name. It is to the company's further credit that it showed respect for the public's intelligence by retaining Tylenol rather than coining another name and pretending the product was a new formulation.

Given the urgency of the situation (Tylenol at the time of its recall accounted for 17 per cent of J&J's corporate profits), it was imperative to repackage and reissue Tylenol as quickly as possible. Working closely with its existing suppliers and a variety of other packagers, J&J considered a number of alternatives, including a fliptop can. In light of the disastrous publicity, the company from the beginning was determined to have a back-up system so that if one seal were broken another would visually articulate product integrity. The exigencies of time ruled out extensive experimentation and it was obvious that the company would have to work within the state of the art. As a consequence, there is nothing new from a creative viewpoint in the packaging solution that was selected. Instead of going with two of the three alternatives it was considering, J&J opted to adopt all of them. Tylenol was reintroduced in a bottle with a seal across its mouth and topped with a cap with solid neckband around its edge. This was then placed in a box whose flaps were glued.

In a sense, this is packaging overkill. But considering the seriousness of the matter, J&J can hardly be faulted for erring on the side of caution. And, in

fairness, it did show good judgment in rejecting the fliptop can, a solution ludicrously inappropriate and excessively expensive.

Perhaps, like "Truth in Packaging" and ordering by console, the safety issue has had its moment. Concern has shifted and the pharmaceutical companies have their attention engaged by moves that might require the listing of ingredients on their packaging. Safety resolved, those concerned with packaging developments are free to look for trends elsewhere.

In the last decade or so, some of the most significant developments in packaging have been of an evolutionary rather than revolutionary character. While cosmic in implication, these have frequently been heralded with little or no fanfare. Unlike such things as the Universal Product Code, which emerged in a glare of publicity only to fade as quickly from the public consciousness, these developments can be read in the context of changing mores and shifting economic priorities.

The trend toward self-service, for example, continues unabated. Products that in the 1960s would have been passed across a counter by a clerk now hang on racks or may be found in floor or wall displays. For a wide array of goods from haberdashery to hosiery, hardware to health care, the knowledgeable package has taken the place of the often inexperienced clerk.

For the package designer, the last several decades have been a period of extraordinary opportunity. Although the halcyon '60s gave us such things as cigarette packs without brand names and beer bottles that doubled as bud vases, it is the recession-ravaged '70s that proved the true test of the designer's mettle. Products as diverse as ice cream and motor oil were packaged with graphic sophistication and structural ingenuity. Elegant containers once the exclusive purview of the carriage-trade stores found their way to supermarket shelves.

It is this cross-fertilization of ideas that underscores the vitality of packaging today. From boutiques to bargain basements, gourmet shops to fast food outlets, the consumer is treated to a level of packaging the technical quality of which is nothing short of perfection. Details previously associated with cosmetics have drifted down to popularly priced items and jewel-like colors may even be found on the packages of dairy products.

Certainly, the news is not restricted to mass markets nor may salesclerks be considered an endangered species. Around the country, small shops are springing up everywhere to cater to the needs of the young, primarily urban, professional. Such places bring the carriage-trade operation full circle, from specialty shop to mass market and back again. Ironically, the packaging for these emporiums, while attractive and evocative, is extremely conventional. There is a reliance on wraps and ties to convey distinction. Stock containers and caps and standard boxes and bags are skillfully disguised to belie their off-the-rack origins.

This is not intended as criticism. In fact, it is simply an acknowledgment of economic realities. Yet it speaks volumes about the visual value of packaging. In this age of increasing anonymity, it is the package that personalizes the product. It must not only carry the brand and the other particulars that constitute the *curriculum vitae* of the product, but it must also convey an aura of the uncommon.

The strident, look-at-me tone of some packages of past years is unlamentedly absent from this Casebook's selections. The refinement here is reminiscent of the nuances always present in great oral traditions. The packages voice the special qualities of the products and draw upon the lexicon of design to make the familiar fresh and the fresh, familiar.

This Casebook's packages are a testament to the esthetic and technical competence of contemporary designers. From cookies to chainsaws, lager to lingerie, the products represent an array of problems. These have been resolved in widely divergent ways.

As in past years, about a third of the selections are in the food category. This is hardly surprising in light of the aggressive marketing practices required for success in this area. It is also not surprising to find that certain trends continue. Images of "down home," with connotations of homemade freshness, remain powerfully appealing. This is an indication of the public's ongoing health consciousness.

Many of the same people for whom this is alluring are also drawn to gourmet foods. Here, the image is decidedly not folksy, although the containers and labels often aim to convey an equally nostalgic feeling, if an upscale one. The image speaks of refinement and selection and is compatible with the premium prices such products command. The idea is that if one demands quality one must expect to pay for it.

It is worth noting in this context that the jurors' selections show little evidence of overpackaging. This seems tacitly to reflect that, while they are willing to pay more, consumers want value and not frills for their money.
— *Barbara and Roger Guilfoyle*

Barry Seelig

Barry Seelig, currently director of corporate design for International Playtex, Inc., received his B.S. in Industrial Design from the Philadelphia College of Art and his M.A. from Wayne State University. He began his career as a designer for the Frigidaire division of General Motors. He has also worked for Walter Dorwin Teague Associates, Estee Lauder and Avon products. Prior to joining Playtex, he was manager of design for Colgate-Palmolive, where he supervised all the packaging and promotion design, including development of a corporate identity program. He is a member of the Industrial Designers Society of America, and on the boards of the Package Designers Council and the American Management Association of Packaging Professionals.

Johanna Bohoy

Johanna Bohoy is art director for the Charrette Corp. of Woburn, Massachusetts, and is responsible for the company's corporate identity program, packaging, promotion, advertising and merchandise display. She received her B.F.A. from Rochester Institute of Technology in 1970, and prior to joining Charrette she was designer for Ginn and Co. Publishing. Bohoy's work has earned recognition from, among others, the Art Directors Clubs of New York and Boston, Boston's Advertising Club, Society of Illustrators, New York Type Directors Club and the *Print Casebooks*. In addition, she is author and illustrator of *The Nothing Zoo*, published by Ginn and Co.

Rei Yoshimura

Rei Yoshimura is a founding principal, with Hiro Komatsu, of XICO, Inc., a cultural/ marketing design firm. Prior to forming XICO, he was principal of his own design firm, Yoshimura and Company. He had previously worked as senior designer for Loewy, Snaith and Lippincott and Margulies. Born and raised in Japan, Yoshimura was educated at the Art Center College of Design in Pasadena, California, and graduated in 1976. His work has been cited for design excellence by the AIGA, Industrial Design magazine, Exhibition One, *Print Casebooks 3, 4* and *5,* and the Type Directors Show.

David Law

David Law is senior vice-president of Vignelli Associates, which he joined in 1978. Prior to that, he was manager of packaging design at J.C. Penney, co-founder of the Design Planning Group in Chicago, and executive designer of Unimark International. Law graduated with honors from Art Center College in Los Angeles in 1961. His clients have included Ford, Gillette, Standard Oil of Indiana, J.C. Penney, Memorex, Sunar and IBM. He has received design awards from the AIGA, the New York Type Directors Club, the Package Designers Council, and Industrial Design Review. His work is also represented in a permanent collection at the Cooper-Hewitt Museum in New York City.

Fred Mittleman

Fred Mittleman is president and creative director of Frederick Mittleman Design Associates, a New York-based consulting firm which specializes in marketing design services. FMDA clients include Bristol-Meyers, Coopers and Lybrand, General Foods, Mobil Chemical, Nestle and Somerset Importers. Prior to founding FMDA, Mittleman's experience included direction of marketing communications and development with Gianninoto Associates and Siebel/Mohr, Inc. A recipient of a number of design awards and honors, he has also written for such publications as Advertising Age and Cosmetic Technology.

Casebook Writers

J. Roger Guilfoyle

Co-authors J. Roger and Barbara Allen Guilfoyle have collaborated on a wide variety of editorial projects, including the last *Best in Packaging*. They have written books, magazine articles, newsletters, brochures and package copy.

They began their collaboration at Industrial Design magazine in the 1960s. Since then, they have worked for a number of consumer and business publications

Barbara A. Guilfoyle

including Cosmopolitan, Good Housekeeping, Sports Illustrated, Interiors and PRINT. Their combined experience also includes motion pictures, television, radio and exhibition credits, with projects for PBS, the Voice of America, and the Smithsonian Institution. They have worked on projects with grants from NEA, NEH, the New York State Council on the Arts, and the Hall Foundation.

Index

Products

A&W Food Service **68**
Abercrombie & Fitch Shopping Bags **56**
Alaska Frozen Fish **44**
Armour Foods Dinner Classics **30**
Atari Computer Hardware & Software **12**
Bigsby & Kruthers Tux Gift Box **33**
Bucilla Needlecraft Kit **46**
Bumble Bee Limited Catch **80**
California Soleil Vineyards **28**
Carnation Dairy Products **50**
Carnation Nutrition Products **48**
Charrette Chop Frames **20**
Charrette Microline Masking Film **20**
Cobraline Automotive Ignition Parts **76**
Crabtree & Evelyn Jams & Jellies **36**
Disston Chain Saw Accessories **52**
Dynamo **70**
Ekco Bakeware **82**
ForPlay Sensual Lubricant **64**
Kaopectate **78**
KHK Pharmaceuticals **38**
L'Aimée Swiss Shower Spa **26**
Lawry's Classic Dressing **10**
Leland Music Cassette **17**
M&Co. Self-Promotion **14**
MacFarms Macadamia Nuts **42**
Melitta Coffee Products **72**
Missoni Fragrance Press Package **34**
Nabisco Dessert Cookies **54**
Perry Ellis Knit Craft Kit **66**
Polaroid Cameras **84**
Ralston Purina Butcher's Blend **74**
Robinson's Baby Foods **58**
Silverado Vodka **24**
Silverwood Creme de la Creme Ice Cream **60**
South Pacific Export Lager **18**
Victorian Pantry Jams & Desserts **62**
Vitaleyes Eye Compress **47**
Vivitar Instant Slide Printer **16**
Warner Brassieres **40**
Westin Hotels Gift Package **86**

Clients

A&W Services of Canada Ltd. **68**
Abercrombie & Fitch **56**
Armour Foods **30**
Armour Handcrafts, Inc. **46**
Atari **12**
Bigsby & Kruthers **33**
Bumble Bee Seafoods **80**
Burren International **66**
California Soleil Vineyards **28**
Carnation Co. **48, 50**
Castle & Cooke, Inc. **80**
Charrette **20**
Cobraline Manufacturing Corp. **76**
Colgate Palmolive **70**
Colman's of Norwich **58**
Disston **52**
Ekco Housewares Co. **82**
Guild Wineries & Distilleries **24**
Inlaks Seafood Corp. **44**
Kyowa Hakko Kogyo Co. Ltd. **38**
L'Aimée Laboratories **26**
Lawry's Foods, Inc. **10**
Leland Music **17**
M&Co. **14**
MacFarms of Hawaii, Inc. **42**
Max Factor **34**
Melitta, Inc. **72**
Morelle Interprises, Inc. **47**
Nabisco Brands **54**
Polaroid **84**
Scarborough & Co. **36**
Silverwood Dairies, Inc. **60**
South Pacific Breweries Ltd. **18**
Timensa **64**
Upjohn Co., The **78**
Victorian Pantry **62**
Vivitar Corp. **16**
Warner's **40**
Westin Hotels **86**

Design Firms
Designers
Art Directors

Photographers
Illustrators
Letterers

Adam, Peter 60
Akagi, Doug 56
Anderson, Jack R. 86
Ash, Stuart 60
Atari Graphic Design Dept. 12
Bass, Saul 10
Bass/Yager & Associates 10
Beck, Martin J. 52, 70
Benes, Michael 84
Berman, Jerry 42
Berman, Layna 12
Berman, Lynn 64
Berta, Elizabeth 24
Boesel, George F.W. 52
Bohoy, Johanna 20
Bokuniewicz, Carol 14
Bowlby, Samuel 68
Brandewie, John 20
Bright & Associates 44, 48, 64
Bright, Keith 48, 64
Bronz, Joel 40
Bronz, Joel, Design, Inc. 40
Brown, Blair 20
Brubaker, Dennis 74
Burns, Cooper, Hynes Ltd. 36
Burns, Richard 56
Campbell Design Associates 16
Campbell, Kathleen 16
Carabetta, Michael 28
Carabetta/Souter Graphic Design 28
Carnase, Tom 70
Carnase, Tom, Design, Inc. 70
Carstens, Dan 30
Cato, Ken 18
Cato, Ken, Design Co. Pty. Ltd. 18
Charrette Design Dept. 20
Cheng, Chuk-Yee 10
Ciulla, Sam 78
Coming Attractions Communication Service 24
Concepcion, Juan 72
Connolly, Peter 46
Cooper, Heather 36
Daugherty, Patrick 47
Dunn, Craig B. 52
East House Enterprises, Inc. 33
Emerson, Karen 42
Eng-Chu, Margie 80
Fesler, Jim 84
Fossella, Gregory, Associates 52, 70
Fukumori, Noreen 42
Gallagher, Don 68
Garza, Laura 82
Gerstman + Meyers, Inc. 72
Gilchrist, Heather 14
GNU Group, The 56
Goldberg, Margorie 58
Gomez, Flavio M. 42

Goodman, Art 10
Gottschalk + Ash International 60
Gould & Associates, Inc. 58
Gould, Jerome 58
Gray, Mary-Gay 68
Haag, John 12
Hadtke, Fred 46
Hain, Robert 46
Hain, Robert, Associates, Inc. 46
Harte Yamashita & Forest 50
Hayes, Adam 66
Hersch, Anita K. 74
Hill, Jane 48
Holloran, Ted 84
Holloway, Les 60
Hom, Frank 40
Hornall, John 86
Hornall, John, Design Works 86
Jonson Pedersen Hinrichs and Shakery 12
Kalman, Tibor 14
Kanei, Norico 66
Kellbach, Jack 78
Kerr, Richard 60
Kleiner, Cindy 48
Kneapler/Daugherty 47
Kneapler, John 47
Krimston, Wayne 30
Kwan, Bill 18
Kysar, Ed 58
Lam, Sy 26
Landi, Rodney 66
Larrick, Jon 44
Lee, Billy 68
Lee, Korte 12
Lipari, Allyn 66
Lister/Butler, Inc. 54, 70, 74
Lister, John 54, 70, 74
Loftus, Kerry G.E. 52
Lopez, Jon 72
Lowry, Scott 34
M&Co. 14
Mabry, Michael 80
Mabry, Michael, Design 80
Maddocks & Co. 26
Mangas, Leslie 78
Mazur, Ron 33
Melvan, Paul 24
Metz, John 82
Meyers, Herbert M. 72
Meyers, Sandra 76
Millen, Morton 54
Moorehouse, Neil 18
Murrie, Herbert L. 30
Murrie White Drummond Lienhart & Associates 30
Neher, John 82
Nevins, James 42
Olsen, Carol 84
Ong, Wilson 62
Perks, Christopher 18

Polaroid Design Dept. 84
Pritchard, Carson 26
Racila, John 82
Racila, John, and Associates 82
Reed, James 56
Reis, Gerald 62
Reis, Gerald, and Co. 62
Rettger, Helen 54
Riddell, Larry 72
Robinson, June 66
Runyon, Richard 24
Samuel Graphic Arts Ltd. 68
Sargent, Peter 48, 64
Sarnoff, Bill 12
Saul, Janice 50
Savitz, Bonnie 70
Schmidt, Nancy 48
Scott, Mary 26
Seelig, Barry 70
Shoptaugh, John 14
Sidjakov Berman & Gomez 42
Sidjakov, Nicolas 42
Souter, Michael 28
Supple, Marylou 20
Taylor, Kathleen 26
Teis, Jane 50
Thompson, Dennis 24
Thompson, Jody Shoults 24
Tomlinson, Bill 84
Vallarta, Frederick Z., Associates, Inc. 78
Van Noy, Ann 34
Van Noy Co., The 34
Van Noy, Jim 34
van Tassel, Joan 26
Voutas, Martha 66
Voutas, Martha, Productions 66
Wallin, Mark 12
Walters, Carol 84
Weller, Don 17
Weller Institute for the Cure of Design, Inc., The 17
Wells, Jay 46
Williams, Sharon 68
Won, Ben 12
Wood, Ray 44, 48, 64
Woodall, Ron 68
XICO, Inc. 38
Yamanouchi, Keisuke 38
Yamashita, Tets 50
Yoshida, Zengo 34
Yoshimura, Rei 38
Ziella, Frank 76

Bass/Yager and Associates 10
Berman, Steve 26
Blakeman, Robert 16
Bull, Michael 42
Bush, Charles William 26
Cheeseman, Karan 60
Christensen, Ron 16
Clark, Tim 48
Crutchfield, Susan 56
DeMilt, Ron 74
Feldman, Marc 48
Gan, Lena 18
Girvin, Tim 80
Grobe, Steve, Photography 84
Hughes, Charles 30
Inouye, Yosh 60
King, Dale 50
Kolze, Larry 30
Kysar, Ed 58
Lennard, Erica 66
Marge, Elias 72
Meyers, Sandra 76
Noonan, Julia 72
Ong, Wilson 62
Pino, Giuseppe 34
Plotkin, Barney 72
Pruitt, David 72
Quinn, Colleen 42
Reis, Gerald 62
Rice, Peter K. 52
Santelli, Sal 72
Schlegel, Robert 54
Sprattler, Rob 50
Vidal, Bernard 47
Walker, Bob 58
Walker, Bruce 56
Wong, Stanley 68
Woodall, Heather 68

Lawry's Classic Dressing

Lawry's Foods and Saul Bass/Herb Yager Associates have been working together for more than 20 years. The design firm's first design for Lawry used the flat-sided bottle with the tapering neck that is now widely accepted in the salad dressing market.

Recently, the designers were asked to create new label and neckband graphics for the existing bottles, which they had designed in 1976. Lawry wanted to update the packaging and change the marketing strategy for the line. Lawry did not want to lose the equity involved in the look of the old bottle, yet it wanted to convey the cachet of "Classic Dressing."

The designers developed a product identification mark for the line by using the existing illustration, while allowing each variety of dressing its own cartouche, lettering style and color. The gold background for the mark and cartouche was added for a rich look to connect the entire line.

Lawry's felt that, by designating the line as "Classic Dressing," it would have the flexibility to add other flavors.

In addition to the gold background, seven other colors were selected to distinguish among the dressing styles. Some of these colors were obvious choices—for example, red was used to indicate red wine vinaigrette.

Opposite: The new mark, top, incorporates the illustration from the 1976 redesign, bottom left. Each dressing flavor is distinguished by color and lettering style and then enclosed in its own cartouche, bottom right. New neckbands provide the corporate umbrella that unites the dressing varieties.

Client: Lawry's Foods, Inc., Los Angeles
Design firm: Saul Bass/Herb Yager and Associates, Los Angeles
Designers: Saul Bass, Art Goodman, Chuk-Yee Cheng
Illustrator: Saul Bass/Herb Yager and Associates
Client liaison: Rob Tribkin, business planning/development

Atari Computer Hardware and Software

Atari had decided to change its hardware packaging from corrugated to SBS with EPS foam capsule. At the same time, the company wanted to establish a uniformity for its software line by using a universal vacuform tray. Consequently, this seemed the appropriate moment to give its packaging graphics a more consistent, upscale, high-tech look.

The aim was to give Atari a competitive edge. The idea was that the packages would convey an image of higher quality and greater technical sophisticaiton.

Atari's packaging manager was in charge of the redesign.

While the structural changes were initiated to reduce the costs, they were also an opportunity to sharpen the company's image. New graphics were dictated by these changes in packaging materials and by the desire to improve Atari's competitive position in the crowded personal computer marketplace.

Several elements were employed to meet the criteria. A silver pinstripe box deliberately alludes to IBM and connotes technical quality. A three-quarter view of the computer highlights the design of the product and heightens Atari's market profile.

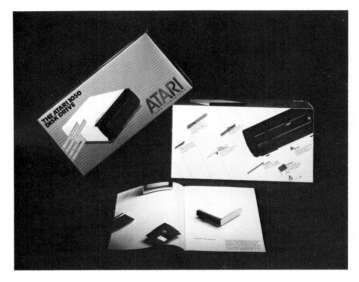

Client: Atari, Inc., San José, CA
Design firm: Jonson Pedersen Hinrichs and Shakery, San Francisco, with Atari Graphic Design Dept.
Designers: Layna Berman, graphic design; Ben Won, graphic design; Mark Wallin, graphic design; Bill Sarnoff, packaging and hardware graphic design manager; John Haag, software graphic design manager; Korte Lee, industrial design
Supplier: Ivy Hill Printing
Client liaisons: Joel Miller, manager, publications and packaging; Bill Sarnoff, packaging and hardware graphic design manager; John Haag, software graphic design manager

The graphics of the package facings are slickly reiterated in the product brochures. The effect of technical virtuosity is designed to project a more powerful image that denotes quality while setting Atari above the competition.

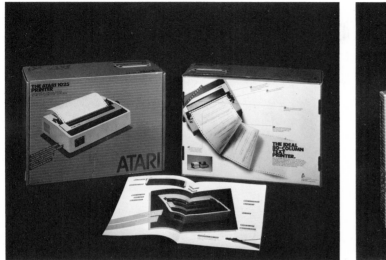

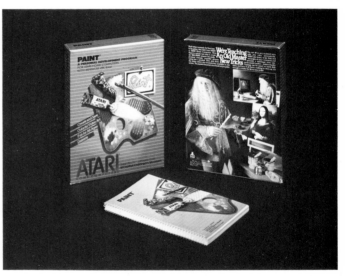

13/Packaging

M&Co.
Self-Promotion

M&Co. set out to do some self-promotion. It had in mind a three-dimensional greeting for clients and friends. The objective was to create an item that would express creativity, project warmth, and have a sense of permanence.

The idea of a box of pencils fit these criteria. The concept of using pencils displayed a sense of whimsy at a time of disposable pens. The wooden box and nostalgic graphics expressed a personal touch too often absent in this impersonal age. The usefulness implicit in the pencils themselves and in the reusable box evinced a concern for everyday cares. The pencils also provided myriad opportunities to promote the design firm's identity.

M&Co. chose to make the box of raw pine. The designers selected this material because they felt it visually enhanced the feeling of warmth. Also, unfinished pine recommended itself because it was reasonably priced. This attention to economy cannot have been lost on clients and potential clients.

Client/design firm: M&Co., New York City
Designers: Tibor Kalman, Carol Bokuniewicz, John Shoptaugh, Heather Gilchrist

The grain of unfinished pine provides a richly textured background for a box of #2 pencils. Warmth and a gentle wit are conveyed by this self-promotion which joins economy of detail to economy of production.

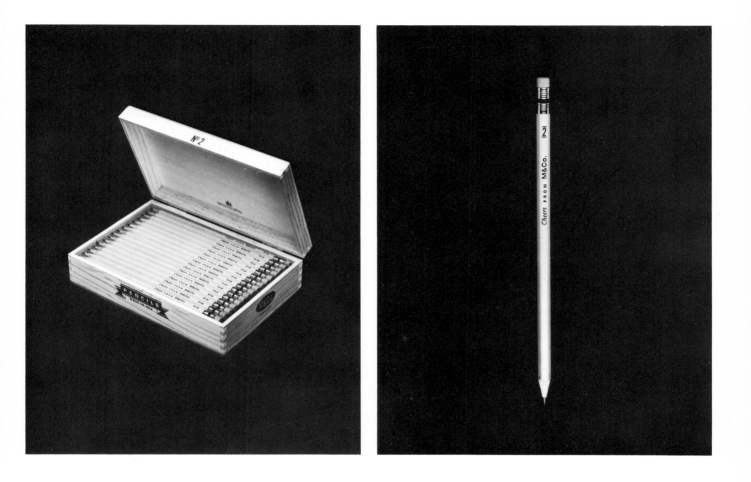

Vivitar Instant Slide Printer

The dilemma for Campbell Design Associates was to create a package for the Vivitar Instant Slide Printer that would graphically articulate its benefits to the user without resorting to verbose explication. This was vital as distribution around the world required copy in English, French, German and Spanish.

Given the sophistication of the market, Vivitar was particularly anxious to stress the high-tech character and professional nature of the product. The package had not only to provoke the consumer's interest but sustain it as well. CDA's solution evoked the language of the darkroom. By juxtaposing the slide to the print it was made from, CDA suggested both quality and facility.

The background provides an especially effective backdrop. Black, with a subtle gray grid pattern, it offers a striking contrast to the photographic images and emphasizes size and clarity in the context of the darkroom.

To keep typography to a minimum, descriptive copy appears on each of the side panels in two of the four languages. The top panel, which carries copy in all four languages, has been reserved for a view of the product itself. All text abuts a colored rule that reiterates the blue background behind the Vivitar logo.

The serious demeanor of the packaging was designed with the demographics of the amateur photographic market in mind. This market is 90 per cent male, with more than half of them over 40 years old and earning more than $50,000.

Client: Vivitar Corp., Santa Monica, CA
Design firm: Campbell Design Associates, Los Angeles
Designer: Kathleen Campbell
Photographers: Ron Christensen (balloon print), Robert Blakeman (girl in room print)
Client liaisons: Dennis Levine, director of marketing; Steve Shull, manager, industrial design

More important than what the product looks like, right, is what it does. Ease of operation and excellence of results are effectively conveyed by the package graphics which transcend the linguistic barriers of the market.

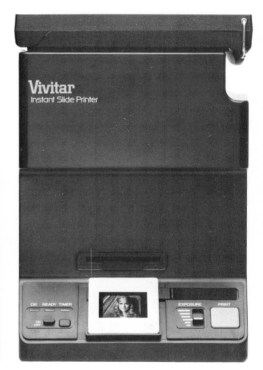

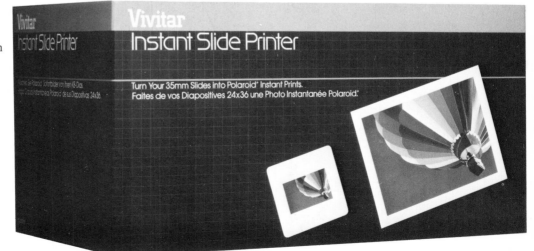

Leland
Music Cassette

Leland Music specializes in songs that have their roots in folk and blues traditions. The company wanted a design that would suggest this visually and be effective for a variety of demos. It was important that this design be easily printed. Equally essential was that it work well in the context of the standard plastic cassette box.

Most commercial cassette package designs are simply extreme reductions of album covers. Most demo tapes are simply labelled with handwritten stickers.

Leland hired Weller Institute for the Cure of Design, Inc., to create a design that would address the problem in general terms, yet be sufficiently distinctive to lift its folk and blues demos out of the competitive pack. The designer proposed a simple graphic solution. Using a silhouette of a musician with a guitar, Weller established a personal, down-home quality for the demos. This was enhanced by the naturalistic image of a bird chirping, with a musical note in the open beak, that Weller created as the corporate mark.

The graphics on these demo cassettes evoke the heartfelt, down-home character of interpretation implicit in blues and folk material.

LELAND MUSIC

Client: Leland Music, Los Angeles
Design firm: The Weller Institute for the Cure of Design, Inc., Los Angeles
Designer: Don Weller
Client liaison: Richard Wedler

17/Packaging

South Pacific
Export Lager

Ken Cato Design was asked to develop packaging for a range of premium quality beers for a brewery based in New Guinea. The aim was to create an image that would enable the client to tap the export market, particularly in the western continental U.S. and Hawaii and Australia.

One of the company's products was "The Beer of Paradise." This beer had a powerful claim to promote. In a product area where endorsements are a primary advertising device, The Beer of Paradise could point to the gold medal it had recently received at the international beer competition.

Given the nature of the target market and its Pacific orientation, the designers drew upon the language of the islands for the label. Associations with bucolic islands of palm trees, white beaches and blue lagoons were conjured up. A bird of paradise provides a burst of color in the foreground. The effect plumbs the stuff of Polynesian legends.

The green glass bottle and white steel can are derived from the green and white corporate colors of South Pacific Brewery. Further, the bottle's color and shape evoke the premium image associated with the best European beers.

Test marketing was done in the Hawaiian Islands. Hawaii was selected for a number of reasons. Among these, it was felt that Hawaii's sizable tourist population provided an excellent cross section of consumers. Another was the geography of the client's operations. South Pacific has a large brewery in Hawaii.

Graphics and color are designed to suggest enchanted evenings gazing across the lagoon to Bali-Hai while sipping South Pacific beer. The premium quality of the product is further enhanced by the green bottle, whose shape alludes to Heineken's.

Client: South Pacific Breweries Ltd.
Design firm: Ken Cato Design Co. Pty. Ltd., Port Moresby, Papua, New Guinea
Designers: Ken Cato, Christopher Perks, Bill Kwan, Neil Moorehouse
Illustrator: Lena Gan
Client liaisons: Bruce Flynn, Ken Webb

Charrette

Charrette Chop Frames

The objective for Charrette's corporate design staff was to develop an identity that would make Charrette's chop frames stand above the competition. Given the fact that chop frames are custom-ordered and cut to specification, most products on the market had little in the way of distinctive packaging. Consequently, it was clear that a creative approach to this problem could go a considerable distance toward establishing Charrette's frames. However, it was also necessary that these products be processed and packaged in-house as inexpensively as possible.

As the basis for the product identity, the designers drew upon ancient Chinese. By associating the "chop" in chop frames with Chinese, a relationship was created with the Chinese image "chop" which connotes a seal of quality.

The second step involved the design of the package itself. Research conducted at the Peabody Museum in Salem, Massachusetts, led to the idea of a wrap which enfolded each piece of the frame. This neatly resolved the problem of packaging a wide range of frames in different sizes and proportions. The basic wrap, fold technique and graphics application remain the same for all.

Packaging for shipping was also required and had to use existing materials. The designers recycled shredded computer paper for use as the packing filler. Pre-printed, existing kraft boxes became the container for bulk shipping. A stamped chopmark on the box was added for identity.

Opposite, top: These sketches illustrate the evolution of the signature block and packaging for Charrette's chop frames. Various Chinese motifs were considered; the final mark and package were deemed particularly appropriate to express handcrafted quality, a quality reinforced by the suggestion of custom packaging.

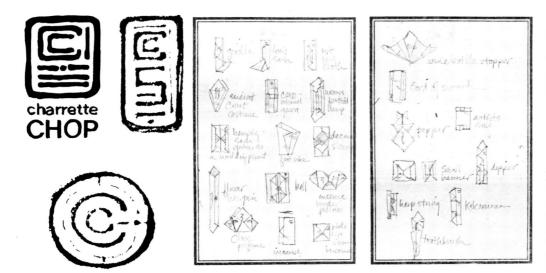

Client: Charrette, Woburn, MA
Design firm: Charrette Design Dept.
Designer: Johanna Bohoy, art
director/designer

Personalizing each frame package is done by the packer. As on oriental wraps, the writing extends from the chopmark. Neat or careful handwriting is not required. The more natural and spontaneous the writing appears, the better, enhancing the custom-made nature of the frames.

Microline Masking Film
Charrette was introducing a line of ruby and amber film. The aim was to develop a package that would bespeak competitive superiority and convey brand quality. This was particularly important as studies in the field of artist's supplies have shown that the brand name was frequently the determining factor in a sale. It was incumbent on the Charrette design team to create an image and package that expressed the professional nature and technical quality of this sophisticated product. Potential customers ran the gamut of the market from graphic designers to printers. It was considered desirable to provide this spectrum of users with a reusable container to store the film.

The designers were originally given an open time frame because the company believed that the importance of the product and market demanded ample research and development. But then the product introduction was advanced to meet a trade show deadline and the package, design and supporting promotional material were needed almost at once. A quick decision had to be made on the design. Fortunately, there were roughs of the alternatives.

The solution hinged on carrier tubes. These were procured from various sources. Rather than silkscreening the tubes, it was decided to use labels. The final elements of the project included a tube, cap, product insert and labeling. All elements were assembled in-house by the processing department. Amber and ruby as well as white were used as the prominent colors to match the product.

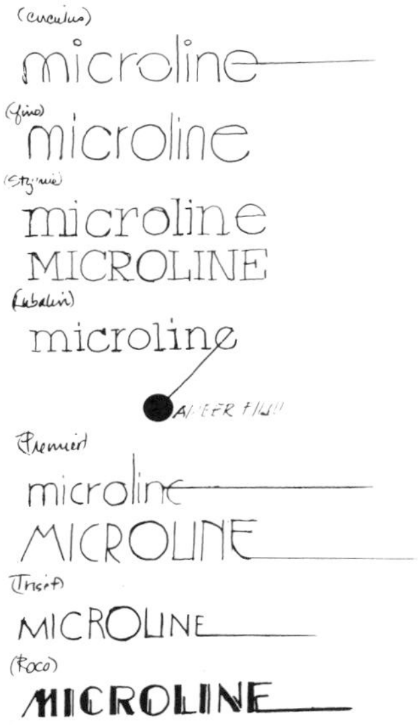

(cursive)
microline

(fine)
microline

(Styrum)
microline

MICROLINE

(kabalin)
microline

AMBER FILM

(Premier)
microline

MICROLINE

(Insert)
MICROLINE

(Poco)
MICROLINE

MICROLINE
RUBY
AND
AMBER
MASKING
FILM

A variety of visual and typographic effects were considered for the labels and caps of film tubes. Ultimately, straightforward lettering was combined with a fluid, abstract form to project technical quality and professional control.

Client: Charrette, Woburn, MA
Design firm: Charrette Design Dept.
Designers: Johanna Bohoy, art director; Johanna Bohoy, Marylou Supple, designers; Blair Brown, John Brandewie, marketing

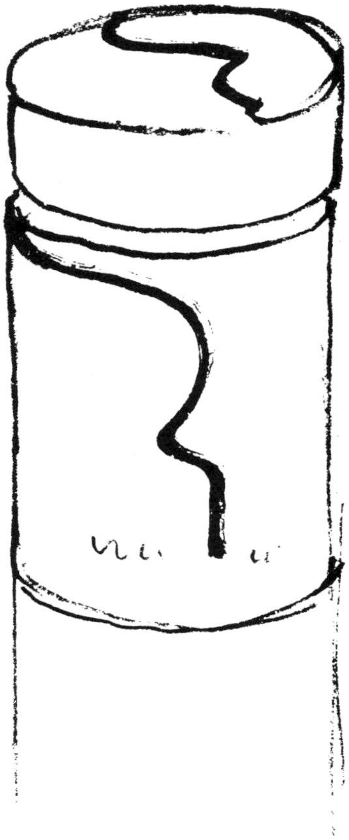

LITH TECH MASKING FILM

charrette amber masking film

charrette amber masking film amber

LITH TECH
AMBER
MASKING FILM

LITH TECH
AMBER
MASKING
FILM

Silverado Vodka

Guild Wineries and Distillers was concerned about the lack of sales for its Silverado vodka. They hired Coming Attractions Communication Service to identify the reasons for this poor performance. CACS was also given the job of developing a new package that would reposition the product.

The designers found a number of reasons for the product's desultory performance. Included in their reading was the bottle shape and style and the label color and design, all of which they felt contributed to the incorrect positioning of the product.

CACS designed a vertically prismed clear-glass bottle with a long chromed-plastic capsule around the neck. The facets on the neck reiterate the bottle shape. The name Silverado runs vertically on one facet along with a winged bird, which was the symbol of the Fort Ross Russian-American Fur Trading Company (Fort Ross having been the early Russian settlement on San Francisco bay). The name and symbol are printed directly in white on the glass by Applied Label Color.

Quality is implicit in the proprietary aspect of the decanter package. This is reinforced by support communications, which position Silverado against such premium vodkas as Absolut, Czar de Smirnoff and Finlandia.

Old

New

Opposite: Before-and-after shots illustrate the repositioning as a quality product of this vodka distilled from California grapes. Left: Chromed plastic capsule covers cap and neck to echo the facets of the glass bottle. Below: Alternative labels and neck treatments that were considered.

Client Guild Wineries & Distilleries, San Francisco
Design firm: Coming Attractions Communication Service, San Francisco
Designers: Jody Shoults Thompson, Dennis Thompson, art directors; Dennis Thompson, Elizabeth Berta, designers; Richard Runyon, Paul Melvan, glass designers
Client liaisons: Joseph Rolla, vice-president, marketing; Mary Hart Thompson, director of creative services
Suppliers: Glass Containers Corp. (bottle mold); RBK Tool & Die Co. (capsule)

L'Aimee Swiss Shower Spa

Maddocks and Company were commissioned to coin a corporate name, develop a brand identity and create a package for a bath/beauty-oriented product. The new product was a skin conditioner with a difference. It was a product which used the shower head as dispenser and provided skin treatment as a natural extension of the cleansing and refreshing experience of a shower.

The user would mix the two liquid elements of the formula, which, by means of a connecting fixture and tube, goes through the shower head and actually comes out with the shower water.

The liquids being dispensed address different needs. The first is a neutralizer which removes soap residue from the skin. The second provides moisturizing treatment to the skin.

The client's expectations included the designers guiding the entire project through from conceptual stage to finished art. The designers were also asked to conduct marketing studies and focus groups.

Maddocks' solution concentrated on the European character of a beauty and skin-care regimen. In creating the name for the company, the designers wanted to convey a continental ambiance. This allusion was not hyperbole, as the client was affiliated with a Swiss laboratory. L'Aimee, the name developed, comes from the French verb "aimer," meaning to like or to love.

For the product name, the designers decided to stress the system or regimen benefits. The result was "Swiss Shower

Above: Comps shown to prospective buyers found their way to the market with minor modifications in color and detail.

Spa," conveying the unusual capacity to dispense liquids directly in the shower water. This, when combined with the company name, met the client's communication goals.

After the names were determined, Maddocks considered typographic treatments. There was a strong feeling that these should say "well-being" in the context of total body-care appeal. It was decided to convey sensuality within the accepted boundaries of good taste.

Because of the physical components, a horizontal package seemed indicated. The concept of a spa environment where one is pampered began to emerge as a dominant theme. This direction allowed the designers to position the body in a horizontal attitude, thereby achieving more dramatic scale with the photography. A tightly cropped torso of a woman enjoying the product became the final direction.

The designers also recommended that the package be designed as its own point-of-purchase display. This approach led to a frame view style of container. The inner lid gave the designers another surface cn which to extol the product's benefits. As the lid is opened, the name of the product is reinforced. The image of an attractive woman visually amplifies the user benefits.

Client: L'Aimee Laboratories, Beverly Hills, CA
Design firm: Maddocks & Co. Beverly Hills, CA
Designers: Mary Scott, creative director/designer; Kathleen Taylor, designer; Carson Pritchard, designer; Sy Lam, design consultant; Joan van Tassel, copywriter
Photographers: Charles William Bush, Steve Berman
Supplier: Southern California Carton Co.
Client liaison: Bart Greenhut, president

California
Soleil Vineyards

The information that appears on wine labels is strictly controlled by law in a number of countries. The aim is to protect not only consumers, but growers as well. The reason for this is obvious: Wine is an important economic commodity to the countries and states in which it is produced.

As a rule of thumb, the more information a wine label contains, the better the wine within the bottle. A label that carries the type of wine, the geographic area of origin, the vineyard and the vintner's name as well as the vintage provides all the information that an oenophile needs to know.

In America, where the ranks of wine drinkers have swelled in the last decade, bland jugs with equally indistinguishable labels have metamorphosed into wines with a character that their labels all too frequently belie. This general problem is compounded by the range of wines bottled in any given year. To complicate this further, certain California varieties, for example, may range in taste from moderately dry to very sweet.

What Michael Carabetta/ Michael Souter Graphic Design have achieved for California Soleil Vineyards of Napa Valley is the creation of a label that meets rigid requirements of a Francophile without aping the antique iconography of French wine labels. The design solution for Soleil's Rieslings is elegantly simple. It reflects the unpretentiousness of the wine itself, which, though moderately priced, has the special appeal of having come from the Napa Valley.

The primary design motif is a sun face taken from an old engraving. This seemed a natural direction for the label to take. Not only does the sun face evoke the name of the vineyard; it also conjures up images laden with the heritage of California.

This illusion is further enhanced by other elements of the design. The neutral background, the subtle, fresh color and the extended typography seemed particularly suited to the wine and its origins. The crispness of a California Riesling finds the ideal expression in the graceful lines of the flute-shaped bottle.

As this is a new product, there are no previous sales figures. Since its introduction, however, sales have reportedly been excellent.

Various sun images and typographic layouts were explored to encapsulate the brand name and region of origin of this wine. The aim was to maintain the communications standards associated with better wines and to avoid the visual redundancies of lesser vintages.

Client: California Soleil Vineyards, Yountville, Napa Valley, CA
Design firm: Michael Carabetta/ Michael Souter Graphic Design, San Francisco
Designers: Michael Carabetta, Michael Souter
Client liaison: Ray Mayer

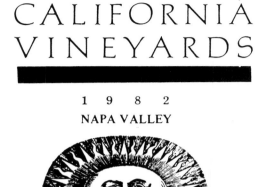

SOLEIL
CALIFORNIA
VINEYARDS

1 9 8 2
NAPA VALLEY

BELLE BLANC

The main purpose of letters is the practical one of making thoughts visible. Ru all letters are frightful things and to be endured only on occasion, that is to sa:

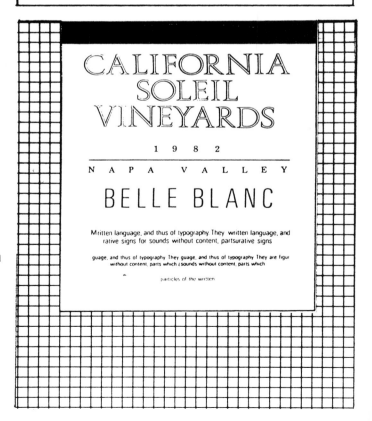

CALIFORNIA
SOLEIL
VINEYARDS

1 9 8 2
NAPA VALLEY
BELLE BLANC

Mritten language, and thus of typography. They written language, and rative signs for sounds without content, partsurative signs

guage, and thus of typography They guage, and thus of typography They are figu without content, parts which zsounds without content, parts which

particles of the written

NAPA VALLEY
CALIFORNIA SOLEIL VINEYARDS
BELLE BLANC
1 9 8 2

cta nam liber tempor cum soluta nobis eligend. Nihil impedit, domir
que civiuda. Et tamen in busdam, neque pecum modot est neque n
ndant. Impro minuit, potius inflammad ut coercend magist at et doc

CALIFORNIA
SOLEIL
VINEYARS
NAPA
VALLEY
1 9 8 2
BELLE BLANC

etters are frightful things and to be endu
laces where the sense of the inscription i
rnament. This is a sweeping statement, l
; yet it is doubtful whether there is art in i
on may be satisfying and in a well comp

CALIFORNIA
SOLEIL
VINEYARDS
NAPA VALLEY
WHITE RIESLING
1 9 8 2

AN OFF DRY WHITE WINE MADE ENTIRELY FROM NAPA VALLEY WHITE RIESLING
GRAPES. PRODUCED AND BOTTLED BY CALIFORNIA SOLEIL VINEYARDS. YOUNT-
VILLE, NAPA VALLEY, CALIFORNIA. ALCOHOL 9.8% BY VOLUME.

Armour Foods
Dinner Classics

Murrie White Drummond Lienhart was commissioned by Armour Foods to provide the graphics for "Dinner Classics," a line of frozen dinner entrees. A completely new category for Armour in the retail market, the product is packaged in a contemporary serving dish especially styled for microwave ovens. The goal of the package design was to promote this feature, while stressing the special quality of the product.

The designers chose a deep brown as the background to highlight appetite appeal. They felt that this approach created a distinctive product billboard in the frozen food section of supermarkets. This character is further emphasized by Palatino Italic, which also modestly suggests the speed of meal preparation.

Dinner Classics was positioned to retail in the premium price range. The idea was to reach customers who desired a better tasting, balanced frozen entree. In addition to promoting a tasty, appetizing dinner, the product photography also serves to highlight the microwave tray's likeness to dinnerware. This immediately distinguishes the product from the competition, which uses paper or foil trays.

Print ads and television spots, following page, use the Dinner Classics packaging to particular effect to imply the gourmet nature of the product.

So good, they belong in the dining room.

Client: Armour Foods, Chicago
Design firm: Murrie White Drummond Lienhart & Associates, Chicago
Designers: Wayne Krimston, design director/designer; Herbert L. Murrie, president; Dan Carstens, vice-president
Calligrapher: Charles Hughes
Photographer: Larry Kolze

Bigsby & Kruthers
Tux Gift Box

This gift box for Chicago retailer Bigsby & Kruthers is part of a coordinated packaging program of bags, boxes and wraps. The shirt box projects the image of a special occasion. Using the language of men's dinner clothes, it is rendered in black-and-white with a touch of red. The effect is a graphic reiteration of a black tuxedo, white dress shirt and red cummerbund.

The special quality offered by the box goes beyond surface allusions, however. The luxe image is affirmed by certain structural innovations. When the top is lifted, the collar style and shirt label are all that is revealed.

The effect of this vignette approach is to focus on the shirt's character as expressed by the collar design. This bespeaks the attention to details long associated with fine tailoring.

The box will accommodate one or two shirts. The dressy image it projects was created specifically with women in mind. As in other areas of men's haberdashery, such as neck and underwear, women are primary purchasers of men's shirts as gifts. The dark, elegant image of men in dinner clothes seemed to evoke the well-tailored vision that most women have of their man.

Client: Bigsby & Kruthers, Chicago
Design firm: East House Enterprises, Inc., New York City
Designer: Ron Mazur, design director
Client liaison: Gene Silverberg

Missoni Fragrance Press Package

Max Factor, in a joint venture with the Italian fashion designers Rosita and Ottavio Missoni, was introducing a chic new fragrance. The clients were attuned to the intensely competitive nature of the scent market. They recognized the importance of capturing the attention of top editors in international women's fashion publications. Careful handling was required to ensure maximum press coverage. It was critical that the press materials convey the luxurious character of Missoni perfume.

Max Factor asked the Van Noy Company to devise a solution that would have the greatest impact within both budget and time requirements. Factor had in mind a four-color product brochure with a slot inside the back cover to accommodate necessary press materials.

The designers advised against this. Instead, Van Noy proposed an elegant portfolio of materials. Central to this was an eight-page brochure, printed in six colors, with an embossed logotype stamped in silver foil. This was to be presented, along with a vial of the fragrance, in a five-color slipcase bound with a cord of Missoni fabric. The slipcase also carried the embossed silver logotype. Van Noy arranged that the press portfolio be delivered to the editors accompanied by a long-stemmed white rose.

The rationale for this was that the introduction of the Missoni fragrance was a news event of such fashion importance that it required something beyond conventional product introduction. The aim was to make the editors feel

singled out for an exclusive preview of Missoni, elegantly packaged as a personal gift.

The brochure and perfume vial were carefully wrapped in matching violet tissue paper to reinforce the gift image. The brochure itself utilized hand-lettered script headlines to futher impart the personal feeling. Photography centered around the Missonis themselves and their fashion creations. The pattern on the slipcase and brochure echoes the perfume's packaging, which was fashioned after one of the Missonis own fabric designs.

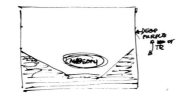

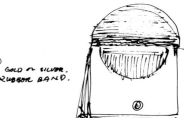

Client: Max Factor, Hollywood, CA
Design firm: The Van Noy Co., Los Angeles
Designers: Jim Van Noy, creative director; Zengo Yoshida, designer; Scott Lowry, production artist; Ann Van Noy, Carol Walters, copywriters
Photographer: Giuseppe Pino
Supplier: George Rice & Sons (printing)
Client liaison: Carol Walters, director of public relations

Early sketches of envelope and folder provide the lineal antecedents of the final design.

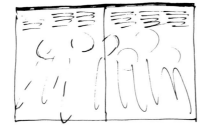

Crabtree & Evelyn
Jams and Jellies

Crabtree & Evelyn is a company whose very name conjures up certain associations. Long successful in specialty food markets, the company has carefully nurtured an image of quality. The logotype itself speaks volumes: Old-fashioned care in the preparation of the product and a sense of concern on the part of the purveyor for the needs of the customer are among the responses that a package of Crabtree & Evelyn evokes. This sense of better things from better times certainly plays to the taste for nostalgia these days, but there is more to Crabtree & Evelyn than *déjà vu.*

Care and attention to details are the hallmarks of the company's remarkable record. The products' packaging seems to flow naturally from one product to the next.

The assignment for Burns, Cooper, Hynes Ltd. was to work with Peter Windett of Windett & Associates, and Cyrus Harvey, president of Crabtree & Evelyn, on a new product introduction. The designers were to develop pictorial images drawn from themes in American genre painting.

Traditionally, Crabtree & Evelyn has had packaging that contained strong allusions to the Old World and the quality inherent therein. An Early American approach was clearly quite a departure for a client who had always relied on English and French motifs.

The designers recognized that it was preeminent that the visual style have taste appeal. It would also have to work well in applications for a wide range of products. BCH and Windett and Harvey ultimately resolved that each product would have a distinctive image.

The labels and paper lids were lithographed from oil-on-board illustrations. All have the fresh, homemade quality associated with the American heartland.

Client: Scarborough & Co., Wilton, NH
Design firm: Burns, Cooper, Hynes Ltd., Toronto
Designer: Heather Cooper
Client liaisons: Peter Windett, president, Peter Windett & Associates; Cyrus Harvey, president, Crabtree & Evelyn Ltd.; Sue Jonas, vice-president and creative director, Scarborough & Co.

KHK
Pharmaceuticals

This assignment involved the redesign of packaging for a line of clinical pharmaceutical products. XICO was originally hired to develop a corporate identity program for Kyowa Hakko Kogyo Co. Ltd., a Japanese conglomerate.

The idea was to create an umbrella for the company's four divisions and their products. The objective was to foster a distinctive brand image for Kyowa's products which would strengthen their market position.

The designers were faced with 27 products of different potencies and in different form from the alcohol, biochemical, food supplement and pharmaceutical products divisions. These were distributed in 3000 separate packages. The feeling was that, by systematically categorizing the products and coherently organizing collateral materials, greater sense could be made of the line for the user.

XICO recommended color-coding as an effective method to bring greater order to the product offerings. Each type and category of medicine would be made clearer in the process. Tablets would be indicated by green; injection ampules, blue; oral medications, orange; and external medications, purple.

As KHK's pharmaceutical products are institutional and not retail, there was a considerable amount of copy. Not only were there directions for use, but explanatory copy as well. For clarity, legibility and a clinical image, a clean white background was used. Legibility was further enhanced by creating a packaging system based on people's natural eye

movements, that is, from left to right, top to bottom, large to small, and light to dark. To ease the doctor's, nurse's and dispenser's task, all product information was laid out on a grid. This emphasized the clinical character of the product line.

Left: Early sketch established the hierarchical approach adapted for this line of clinical products.

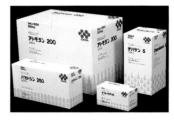

Client: Kyowa Hakko Kogyo Co. Ltd., Tokyo
Design firm: XICO, Inc., New York City
Designers: Rei Yoshimura, design director; Keisuke Yamanouchi, designer
Supplier: Taro Yamashita
Client liaisons: Shigeru Fukuma, manager, public relations; Toshio Osa, director/advertising

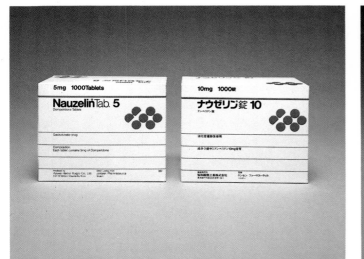

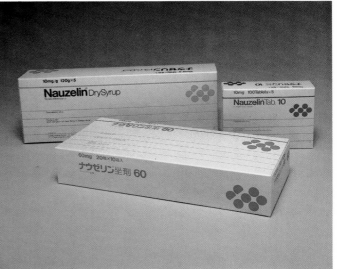

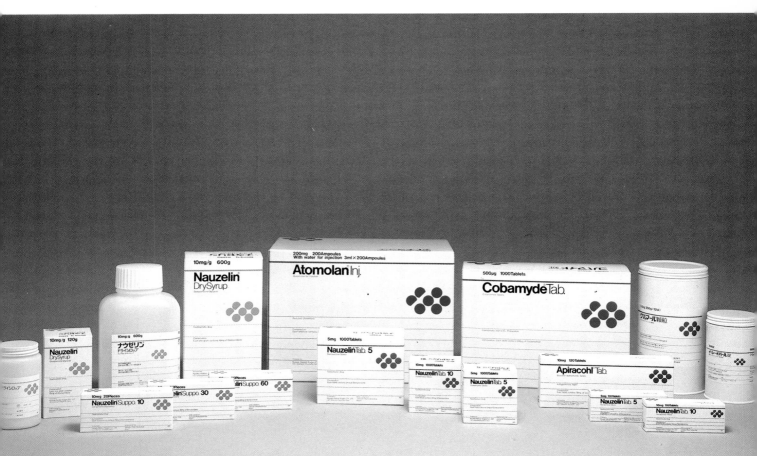

Warner Brassieres

Women's undergarments and plastic hangers seem locked in an embrace. Wherever lingerie is sold, bras and girdles hang precariously from one side or the other of the hanger; hang, that is, until the customer reaches out to select one. Then the article in question either falls to the floor or becomes permanently enmeshed in the rack.

Warner's, a division of the Warnaco Group, had been attempting to resolve the problem of packaging and promoting bras and girdles for several seasons. Packaging alternatives to the system of free-hanging garments on floor racks generally require a shelf display against a wall. Clear packages, which are popular for this category of goods, are often ganged at point-of-purchase. This minimizes visibility.

Warner's was looking for a package that would use existing racks to better advantage and appear more organized. It was also looking for substantially more brand and product identity.

Joel Bronz Design helped resolve Warner's problem by creating packaging with a wraparound die-cut hook at the corner of the package. This not

Sketches, opposite, illustrate the path traveled between the former lackluster package, far left, and the new, more dramatic one. Photo has been reduced in area and treated as just one element in the larger scheme, which includes innovative die-cut hanger hook.

only provided the package with the strength to withstand repeated removal and rehanging; it also resulted in a diamond package configuration. This is unique in the industry. Consequently, it provides Warner's the strong brand identity it wanted.

The designers used soft, feminine colors. These help sustain the mood of the product category. Copy was kept simple and color-keyed to the soft coloring of the package's side panels.

Designers: Frank Hom, Joel Bronz
Supplier: Rexham Packaging (printing)
Client liaisons: Mary Kay Edwards, vice-president, director of advertising; Jesse R. Abboud, vice-president, director of merchandising
Client: Warner's, Bridgeport, CT
Design firm: Joel Bronz Design, Inc., New York City

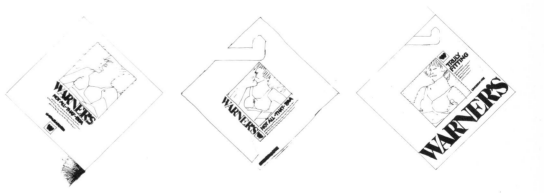

MacFarms
Macadamia Nuts

MacFarms of Hawaii, one of the world's largest producers of macadamia nuts, had previously marketed their product solely through wholesale channels. Consequently, with the decision to enter the retail market, the company felt the need for a brand image to be expressed by a comprehensive packaging system.

The assignment for Sidjakov Berman & Gomez was to develop an image based on a variety of considerations. It was obviously advantageous to visually reinforce the Hawaiian origins of the product. This would support the premium price of macadamia nuts vis-a-vis other nut products.

The product was to be marketed in nitrogen-flushed foil pouches, a packaging technique new to the macadamia nut market. This technique would give MacFarms a slight price advantage over existing macadamia nut brands. However, although lower than its competition in cost, the MacFarms product remained within the premium price structure. Therefore, it was important to employ imagery that evoked quality.

SB&J created a brand image that utilizes a color illustration of a macadamia nut orchard and a line map of the Hawaiian Islands. Both these elements emphasize the origins of the product. The style of the illustrations is intended to create a quality impression and set the brand above the competition. The background motif is a butternut yellow with thin gold stripes. The overall design, while strongly communicating the Hawaiian origins of the product, avoids

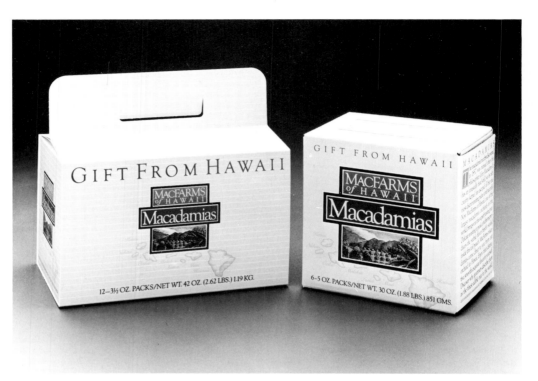

the clichés associated with the islands.

The designers focussed on typefaces that would complement this illustrative approach. Goudy Old Style was selected for the brand and product name, with Snell Roundhand used for the island names.

The design is also applied to the cardboard caddy that provides a convenient display unit for retailers. A cardboard sleeve permits the caddy to double as a gift package/carrying case. On the caddy and sleeve, the stripes are white against the butternut background.

SB&G also created a sales promotion kit directed toward food brokers as well as introductory consumer advertising. The design program has since been extended to corporate identity elements for MacFarms.

Evoking the sun-drenched atmosphere of Hawaii, the warm yellow pouches and boxes effectively combine line art and color. A map of the islands, below graphically establishes the locale, while the multi-color illustration of the Hawaiian landscape, opposite lower left, clearly suggests lush, paradisical growing conditions. The traditional typefaces provide a bridge for a product moving from the wholesale to retail market. As this is the first instance of foil pouches being used for macadamia nuts, the package plays an important role in the advertising, opposite lower right.

Client: MacFarms of Hawaii, Inc., Captain Cook, HI
Design firm: Sidjakov Berman & Gomez, San Francisco
Designers: Flavio M. Gomez, account executive; Nicolas Sidjakov and Jerry Berman, art directors; James Nevins, designer; Karen Emerson, production/design assistance; Noreen Fukumori, production/design assistance
Illustrators: Michael Bull, Colleen Quinn
Client liaisons: Rick Vidgen, vice-president/commercial; Lance O'Connor, vice-president/marketing; Watson Clifford, manager, technical marketing services; Bill Gaydon, manager, sales
Suppliers: Omnicomp, typographers; Ludlow Flexible Packaging, printer (pouch); Kramer Karton Co., printer (caddy)

Alaska
Frozen Fish

The assignment for Bright & Associates was to position the new Alaska Frozen Fish Division of Inlaks Seafood Corporation in the market. This was to be done by creating a memorable image for the company and by developing packaging that would project product quality. The name "Alaska Brands" was devised to convey the nature of the company as a supplier of premium fish products to the restaurant and institutional market.

Bright developed a solution that drew upon familiar references to evoke the traditional values of the marketplace. Engravings of fish were used for cod, jumbo cod, and pollack, and a vignette of an iceberg and fishing trawler for white fish and other species. These illustrations are superimposed on a circular design element, reminiscent of a porthole, that is used for color-coding. The beige package background, with its diagonal lines, suggests wood planking.

The packaging with its simple and direct graphics enabled Alaska Brands to quickly establish its new products with restaurant and institutional buyers. The designers also designed sales and promotional literature and a press kit for the new product.

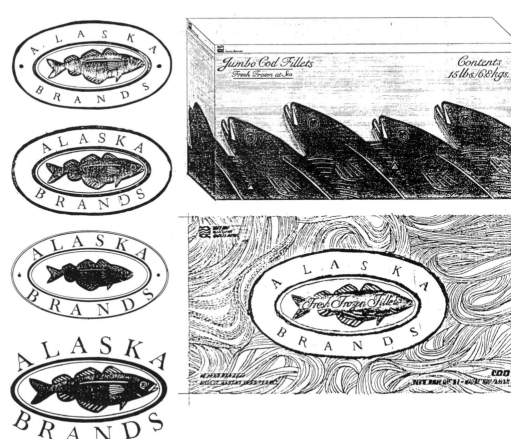

Early comps featured a cameo treatment of a fish against a variety of backgrounds. Such nautical motifs as rough-hewn boards and swirling seascapes were considered. Other design alternatives used the image of leaping, snapping fish. The final design, opposite, kept the fish vignette but superimposed it over a circular device evocative of a porthole. The linear treatment of the background suggests deck planking.

Client: Inlaks Seafood Corp., Seattle
Design firm: Bright & Associates, Los Angeles
Designers: Jon Larrick, Ray Wood
Supplier: Ridgeway Packaging
Client liaison: Assen Nicolov, president

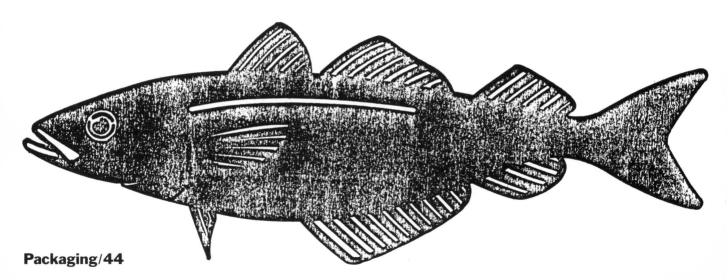

Bucilla
Needlecraft Kit

Bucilla Needlecraft had a twofold objective. First, it desired packaging whose graphics would convey a stronger brand awareness. Second, it was anxious to reduce its existing packaging and manufacturing costs.

Robert Hain Design Associates proposed a bold, yet highly organized graphic system. The idea was to give the product maximum shelf impact. Hain boxed the needlecraft kit, providing the consumer with an "in use" storage structure. This approach is unique to Bucilla, setting its product above the competition.

This concept was also cost-effective. Hain was able to lower the manufacturing expenses for the 1500-item product line. Economies were achieved in the assembly of the various package components.

The new packaging reversed the trend in declining sales. Bucilla's kits increased in sales by 30 per cent. Equally important, the packaging enabled Bucilla to gain more shelf space for its products.

Boxlike display converts into a convenient carry-all bag for needle-point projects.

Client: Armour Handcrafts, Inc., Secaucus, NJ
Design firm: Robert Hain Associates, Inc., Scotch Plains, NJ
Designers: Robert Hain, Fred Hadtke, Jay Wells, Peter Connolly

Vitaleyes
Eye Compress

The product was a new entry in the personal care market. It would be sold in the fiercely competitive environment of the cosmetic counter. The client intended to introduce it in the New York City market, specifically Manhattan. Consequently, it was critical to gain acceptance by such stores as Macy's, Saks Fifth Avenue and Lord & Taylor.

Kneapler/Daugherty were hired to address a range of problems dealing with product presentation. The client clearly was in need of an upscale, sophisticated look to penetrate the projected market. Kneapler/Daugherty had to create a package that would be both a durable shipper and glamorous display. They were also responsible for refining the design details of the product itself.

The client wanted to use the color scheme of black and pink. While these colors are frequently associated with punk culture, they also have a long and strong tradition in the fashion and cosmetic industries.

The nature of the product, an eye compress, and the client's expectations for it suggested a specific approach. A long, slender package shape was chosen for its luxurious and elegant appeal. The designers felt that black was the natural color to evoke both these images. A picture of the product in use was felt to be the most effective way to provoke consumer interest and the most direct way to tell the product's story.

The logo "Vitaleyes" was the most difficult part of the assignment. The client wanted a classical and soft feeling for

the package and proposed a visual separation between the words "vital" and "eyes." The designers were able to pursuade the client on the merits of the elision, Vitaleyes. After many typeface explorations, K/D selected Caslon and convinced the client that a combination of roman and italic faces would create the desired effect. Eras Light typeface was selected for the package copy for its futuristic, readable quality.

The result is a distinctive package that conveys glamor in the context of the contemporary cosmetic counter. There are permutations of both beauty and health care.

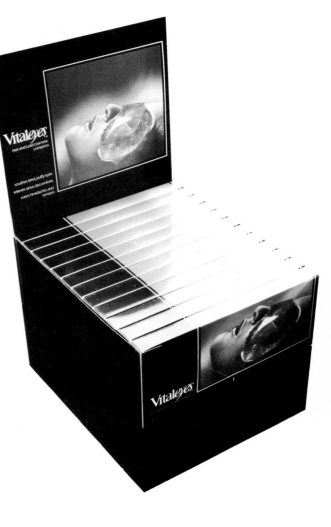

Client: Morelle Interprises, Inc., New York City
Design firm: Kneapler/Daugherty, New York City
Designers: Patrick Daugherty, John Kneapler
Photographer: Bernard Vidal
Client liaison: Michele Donohue, president

Display enhances the glamor posture of the glossy black and pink package to convey the fashion image appropriate to the department store cosmetic counter.

Carnation Nutrition Products

In 1982, Carnation perceived that nutritional and weight-loss packaged foods and vitamins represented an underdeveloped market, particularly in the context of special nutrition centers. The company formed a Health and Nutrition Division to explore this idea through several prototype stores in the Los Angeles area. If successful, the stores would be rolled out nationally.

The nutrition centers were to shelter two separate concepts in one location. A membership-only weight reduction center would be worked out side by side with a retail nutritional foods and vitamin store. The target audience for both of these was seen as 70 per cent of American consumers. This is the segment of the population identified as being weight-conscious and fitness-oriented without being health food enthusiasts. Nor do these people participate in any structured weight-loss program.

In this context, Carnation's Health and Nutrition Division saw the advantages of creating a mainstream environment where customers purchase healthy, low-calorie foods that would be both appealing and good-tasting. This environment was to be created specifically by product packaging and store design. Throughout the project, Bright & Associates worked with Doody Company, store designers, to coordinate the total look of the store.

The two vitamin lines, a Carnation synthetic brand and the premium Good Nature natural brand, were to occupy about 25 per cent of the retail shelf space. Carnation stressed that the two lines be distinctive yet compatible with each other and the other products in the store. Due to the captive nature of the store environment, shelf impact was not considered of primary importance. Priority was given to clearly designating the over 250 items and projecting a quality feeling.

For the Carnation brand, the overall look of packaging is clean and ethical. Bright combined crisp typography with horizontal rules to clarify the various levels of information. The rules, which are graduated in weight, also carry color-coding. Caslon 471 was chosen as the principal typeface to provide a look of sophistication and lend credibility to the synthetic vitamins. On the protein powders, photography was incorporated for appetite appeal and flavor designation.

For the Good Nature line, a contemporary wheat symbol is used to convey a quality natural look. Its circular design has a seal or stamp-like quality. For Good Nature, Bright selected Garamond Old Style italic as principal typeface. Multipack vitamin boxes incorporate stylized illustrations to identify specific vitamin purchases.

Color played an important role in both the Carnation and Good Nature designs. With the Carnation brand, a white background projects the clean, ethical look. The rich colors, used for color-coding, give the line a bright, fresh feeling. In the Good Nature line, a beige background with a subtle grid contributes to the contemporary, natural look. White, orange and deep brown were used in the symbol to give the package label freshness and dimension.

Both Carnation and Good Nature use the same polystyrene bottles. This was done for overall compatibility and inventory purposes. Labels for both were printed offset and then applied.

Client: Carnation Co., Los Angeles
Design firm: Bright & Associates, Los Angeles
Designers: Keith Bright, Ray Wood, Peter Sargent, Cindy Kleiner, Jane Hill, Nancy Schmidt
Illustrator: Tim Clark
Photographer: Marc Feldman
Supplier: ColorGraphics
Client liaisons: Ken Chane, vice-president, Health & Nutrition Div.; Greg Mazares, marketing director, Health & Nutrition Div.; Melissa Urbank, marketing assistant

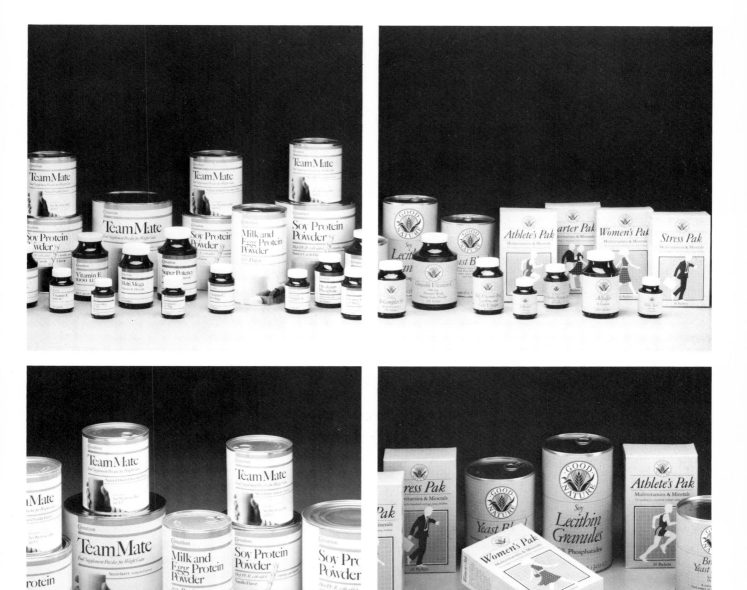

Opposite: Preliminary symbols and labels established the packaging direction and were adopted, with modification, for the final design.

Carnation Dairy Products

The assignment for Harte Yamashita & Forest was to develop a contemporary packaging system for the Carnation line of ice cream products. As the client was committed to cylindrical cartons, one of the traditional shapes associated with ice cream packaging, the problem was essentially a graphic one.

The designers were given the mandate to create a distinctive competitive posture. The object was to enhance the consumer's perception of a family of frozen dairy dessert products, without blurring the distinctions between ice cream and ice milk, and ice milk and sherbet. This was eventually achieved by color-coding.

While HY & F were conducting research and a market survey, Carnation was reevaluating its entire fresh milk and ice cream division packaging. The decision had been made to include all dairy products under the new title "Carnation Dairies" so as to convey a coherent image of quality.

Carnation believed that this umbrella designation would more effectively communicate the nature of the products. The goal was to strengthen the consumer impulse by graphically reinforcing the family look. Given the competitive pressure in the dairy market, Carnation had correctly identified the value of a cohesive image in eliciting positive consumer response.

Harte Yamashita & Forest proposed a solution that broke with some dairy market traditions. The designers played against the industry's tendency to use strong color for ice cream products. With this in mind, they created a line primarily in white with evocative line illustrations. Drawings were made from photographs of scenes at Carnation farms in Carnation, Washington, and Oconomowoc, Wisconsin, circa 1910.

The thinking was that, within the refrigerated cases, this clean, white image would project the refreshing aspect of Carnation ice cream products. An interesting aspect of this approach is that it required the corporate image of a white logotype on a red field be reversed. A red "Carnation" replaced the traditional treatment.

Carnation was so delighted with this that the design was extended to a variety of corporate applications. A manual was created to govern use on stationery, vehicles and uniforms.

Line illustrations evoke a barnyard ambience to connote farm-fresh quality for Carnation dairy products. These illustrations have the additional advantage of printing well on standard paperboard container shapes, enabling Carnation to effectively update its previous packaging, below left.

Client: Carnation Co., Los Angeles
Design firm: Harte Yamashita & Forest, Los Angeles
Designers: Tets Yamashita, creative director; Janice Saul, senior designer; Jane Teis, production
Illustrators: Rob Sprattler, Dale King
Client liaison: Lewis Paine, director of marketing

Disston Chain Saw Accessories

The assignment for Gregory Fossella Design Associates was to develop a merchandising system that would build a market presence for Disston. The idea was to associate the Disston name with chain-saw accessories at point-of-purchase. The aim of the packaging was to simplify the process of matching the correct chains and bars to the appropriate make and model saw.

It was important that the packaging sell itself, as Disston had determined that the firewood and forestry line would not be backed by major advertising budgets. It was essential, therefore, that the packaging lift the line above the competition and project a visually recognizable image of a complete line in the mass-merchandising environment.

To reflect quality and to accentuate the connection with Disston's traditional tool and accessory line packages, black was used for the background. Bold, full-color photography of stacked firewood provided a memorable package identity, while reinforcing the end use of the accessories. This theme was carried through on all the packaging.

Wraparound stickers on the chain bar and saw chain packages enabled Disston to minimize runs. The stickers have a code number on front and a complete listing of saw model numbers on the back for a cross-reference. A point-of-purchase header listed all saws and the code number of bars and chains that would fit each.

Bars were color-coded. Silver type indicates high performance; orange type describes standard bars. The color-coding was also carried through to a symbol on the bar that was developed to build awareness of the roller sprocket nose feature of the Disston bars.

Below: Computer-generated drawing of saw blade package.

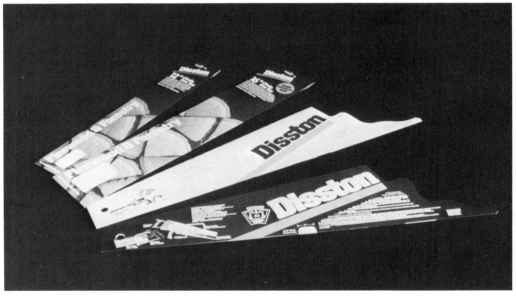

Client: Disston, Greensboro, NC
Design firm: Gregory Fossella Associates, Boston
Designers: Martin J. Beck, creative director; George F.W. Boesel, group design director/packaging designer; Kerry G.F. Loftus, assistant designer; Craig B. Dunn, collateral designer
Photographer: Peter K. Rice
Supplier: Container Corporation of America; P.W. Lewis, structural designer
Client liaisons: George E. King, senior vice-president/sales; Don C. Andrus, director/marketing; Jean Butcher, advertising manager

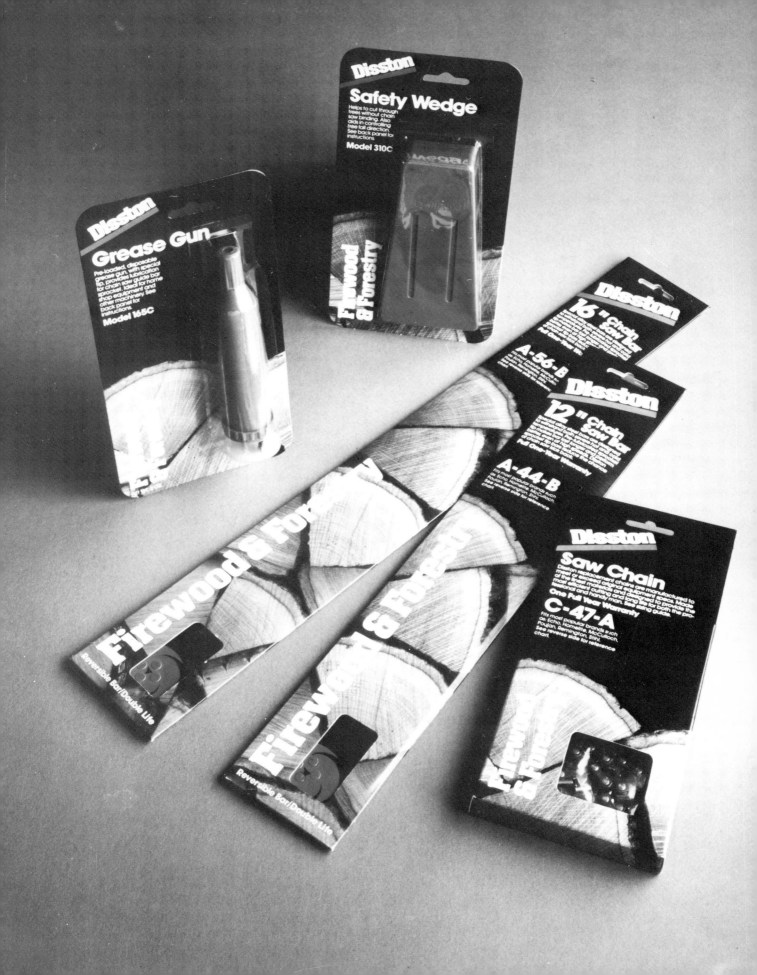

Nabisco Dessert Cookies

Several Nabisco cookies were not reaching the target customer. Priced at a premium, they were created to appeal to those with a more sophisticated palate. Yet they seemed to be having difficulty capturing this market. Nabisco decided that the packaging and promotional materials could be improved to more effectively encourage sales.

Based on the success of Lister/Butler's work on its chocolate line of cookies, Nabisco asked the design firm to develop new packaging for these upscale brands. The designers recommended a unified line of packages, the total impact of which would be greater than that of its constituent parts.

The challenge was to design a graphic system that would position the cookies as luxury products for adults, cookies worth the higher price they commanded. The designers coined new names for several of the products and the term "Dessert Cookies," to suggest that they're not only a delicious treat but also an elegant sweet for guests.

Simple, classic graphics on a gold-colored background immediately convey this. Further, the unified color scheme achieves dramatic shelf impact. Promotional money spent on one product, therefore, benefits the entire line.

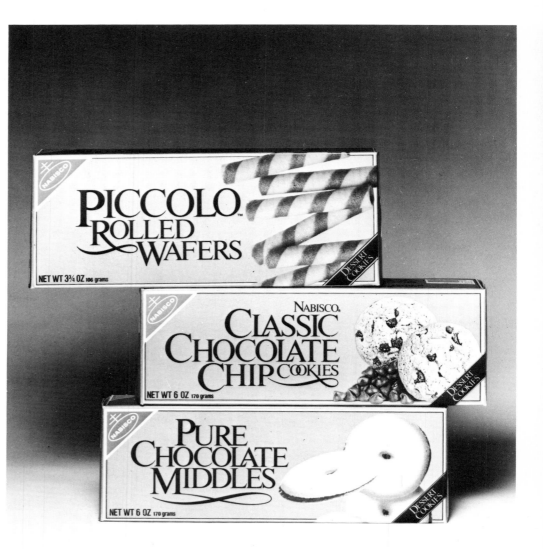

One of the primary aims of the redesign was to make all the facings equally effective at point-of-sale to accommodate to the vagaries of supermarket stacking.

Client: Nabisco Brands, East Hanover, NJ
Design firm: Lister/Butler, Inc., New York City
Designers: John Lister, design director; Helen Rettger, designer; Morton Millen, designer
Photographer: Robert Schlegel
Client liaisons: John DiBlanco, group brand manager; Joseph Simrany, brand manager

Abercrombie & Fitch
Shopping Bags

When Abercrombie & Fitch closed the doors of its Madison Avenue store across from Tripler's and up the street from Brooks Brothers, an era seemed to have ended. Long a purveyor of expensive and esoteric sports equipment to the carriage trade, A&F seemed to be a victim of jet lag, unable to adjust to changing times. With a clientele associated with tweeds and woody station wagons, A&F belonged to the vanished world celebrated in certain New Yorker cartoons. Just as its neighbor, the Biltmore Hotel, long the mecca of buttoned-down collegians, failed to make the transition between the preppy days of yore and *The Preppy Handbook* attitudes of the 1980s, A&F had continued in its role as an outfitter for mundane and exotic sports/ hunting excursions when all most people were taking on safari was a Nikon.

Although A&F discontinued its retail efforts, it did continue as a catalog operation. In one of those ironic twists associated with fickle fashion, A&F became competitively stronger as public taste turned once again to the quality levels represented on its catalog pages. Consequently, as its position as a merchandiser of fine sports goods was reaffirmed, A&F turned its attention again toward retail store operation.

Eventually, A&F reopened its doors. This time, however, it was situated far from the gray flannel world of New York City's Madison Avenue and closer to the exotic world of legend. A&F decided that the gilded streets of Beverly Hills were

the ideal purview for its high-priced, quality line.

To create a packaging image that would effectively convey the essence of its new operation, A&F hired the GNU Group. The idea was to extol the new A&F without losing the context of the old one.

Although A&F was in effect opening a new store in a time and place far removed from its past associations, GNU, nonetheless, felt that big-game motifs would be the most appropriate and evocative image. A&F, after all, had originally opened as a chain catering to gentlemen about to embark on safari.

GNU Group's shopping bag designs derived from animal hides. Leopard spots, tiger and zebra stripes are used for a contemporary fashion image. Cropped and blown up, these motifs have a powerful graphic impact. The images say sport safari without focusing on hunting.

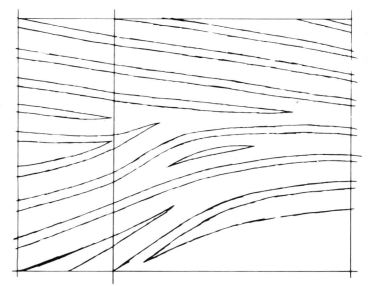

The first rough, right, established design direction and with slight refinements became one of the bag patterns.

Client: Abercrombie & Fitch, Beverly Hills, CA
Design firm: The GNU Group, Sausalito, CA
Designers: Richard Burns, Doug Akagi, James Reed, art directors; James Reed, Doug Akagi, designers
Illustrators: Susan Crutchfield, Bruce Walker
Client liaison: Judy Blake

Robinson's Baby Foods

Robinson's Baby Foods, a division of Colman Foods of Norwich, England, wanted to increase its share of the dry foods sector of the baby foods market. This is not surprising, as dry foods represent 60 per cent of all consumption, with wet foods accounting for the rest.

Robinson's was prompted to redesign its packaging by the losses it incurred to an aggressive German company. This company's packaging had several powerful elements, including appetizing still-life photography and effective color-coding. The Robinson's packaging, on the other hand, featured old-fashioned storybook-style illustrations of babies in various activities.

Gould & Associates was given the assignment to redesign the complete line of over 40 packages. The aim was to motivate consumers by providing visual impact at point-of-sale.

Gould recognized the value of emphasizing the Robinson name. The company, after all, had more than a century of equity invested in it.

Gould's solution was threefold. First, given the strong public identification with the name, an updated version of Robinson's original logotype was developed. Second, to enhance appetite-appeal, a visual emphasis was placed on the ingredients. Ingredients are shown in a natural state to convey a fresh, wholesome image.

These were depicted within a silhouette form that established food categories. A fowl or animal silhouette was developed for meat products; and fruit or vegetable shapes were used where appropriate, while recognizable baby-toy shapes were applied in other areas.

Finally, by centering the particular shilhouettes on the facing of a white box, the designers achieved a strong repeat pattern. Each design works as a little poster.

Based on the success of its new food packaging, Robinson's recently extended the design to its line of baby fruit drinks.

Client: Colman's of Norwich, England
Design firm: Gould & Associates, Inc., Los Angeles
Designers: Jerome Gould, art director; Ed Kysar, art director/designer; Margorie Goldberg, production
Illustrator: Ed Kysar
Photographer: Bob Walker
Client liaison: Roger Northway, marketing controller, Baby Foods Div.

Preliminary sketches, above far left, set the basic approach of using primitive silhouettes as the backdrop for presentation of appetizing, fresh ingredients.

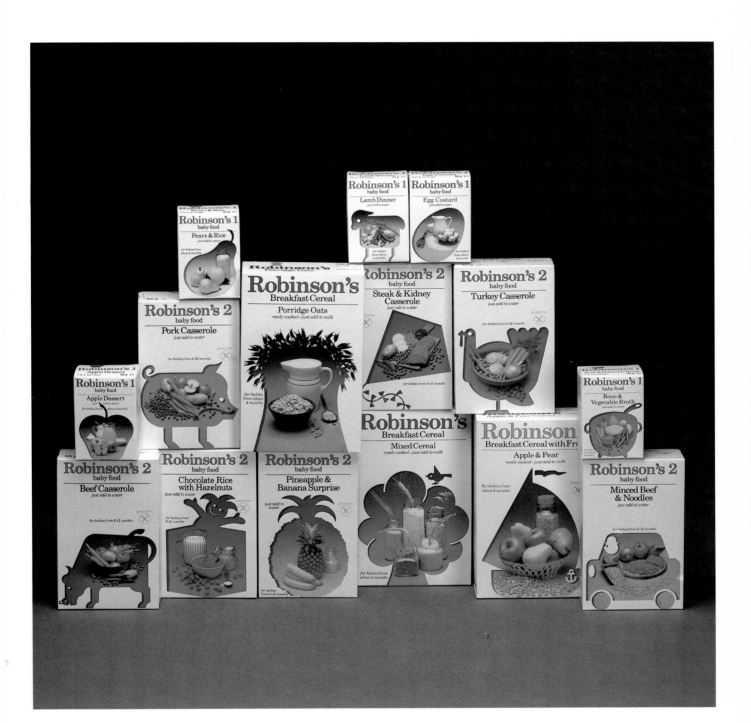

Silverwood Creme de la Creme Ice Cream

Silverwood Dairies wanted to dramatize the quality of its new line of ice cream and hit upon a daring way to do it. Breaking with existing practices, the company decided to price its new ice cream products according to the cost of the constituents required for a particular flavor. This resulted in a three-tiered price structure.

Gottschalk + Ash were hired to create a packaging program that would effectively articulate this hierarchy and represent its value to the consumer. Given the emphasis on the special character of ingredients, G + A felt that the packaging had to capture the cachet of the product, called Creme de la Creme.

This name was chosen for a number of reasons. Obviously, it conveyed the best quality, but it also successfully addressed the bilingual requirements of the Quebec market without patronizing the consumers fluent in either language.

G + A drew upon existing vocabularies of form and color to express the distinctions of cost and taste among flavors. For example, the designers chose the grammar of medals—gold, silver and bronze—to elucidate the three-tiered price structure. This medallion character was also evident in the oval label chosen to establish brand identity.

Dark brown was selected as the background color for its implication of the richness intrinsic in all the Creme de la Creme flavors. Color, drawn from a spectrum of colors, was also used to differentiate the 15 flavors. A color-coordinated wraparound band on the outside was matched to the flavor

Taste was evoked by a closeup photograph representing a soupçon of the contents.

G + A specified one- and two-liter Convocan containers. These were selected for production facility. They require less storage space because the container is assembled from a printed flat right at the plant and then filled.

Client: Silverwood Dairies, Inc., Don Mills, Ontario
Design firm: Gottschalk + Ash International, Toronto
Designers: Stuart Ash, Les Holloway, Richard Kerr, Peter Adam
Lettering: Karan Cheeseman
Photographer: Yosh Inouye
Client liaisons: Scott Findlay, product manager, Frozen Products; Jerry Duncan, director, Sales and Marketing
Supplier: Somerville Belkin Industries

Victorian Pantry
Jams and Desserts

Victorian Pantry approached Gerald Reis and Company to develop packaging for a new line of jams and jellies. The client wanted packaging and labeling that would convey the personal, hand-made quality of its line. It wanted to orient the product to the gift and gourmet food market.

When Victorian Pantry turned to GR&Co., it was still developing its products. This allowed ample time for the design of the labels and packaging. This lead time was crucial. The gourmet market is increasingly more competitive. Effective packaging is vital to attaining a proper market niche.

GR&Co. drew upon a complex palette of rich and muted colors for the design. The rich colors used in the fruits and borders vibrate against the more muted background. This approach was favored over alternative Victorian motifs.

The labels are printed on uncoated matte paper. This evokes the somber sensibility of the Victorian age, a period in which people demanded value for their money.

Soft, gauzy colors of the labels, opposite far right, conjure up images of hand-tinted Victorian pictures. Latticework background provides a strong graphic motif, while conveying the ambiance of a garden.

Client: Victorian Pantry, Saratoga, CA
Design firm: Gerald Reis & Co., San Francisco
Designers/illustrators: Gerald Reis, Wilson Ong
Client liaisons: Dale Bentson, Diane Rogalski

ForPlay Sensual Lubricant

The assignment for Bright + Associates was to develop a name, container and packaging for a personal lubricant product. The goal was to project a credible, quality, "fun" image to the target audience, primarily homosexual men. Since the advertising budget was limited, the package had to be able to generate impulse purchases in both adult boutiques and independent drug chains.

The designers used bright, primary colors in free-form shapes. These were embossed for a three-dimensional effect and then gloss varnished. This provided them with a wet paint look, particularly against a dull varnished gray background. A grid was introduced in the background to suggest ceramic tile.

Typography was kept simple, direct and clean, so as not to clash with the more colorful and playful character of the graphics. The typographic approach was designed to reinforce an image of quality.

Bright selected gray to add sophistication and provide a neutral background for the graphics and type. The bright colors used to project a playful image, when combined with the gray background and white type, are particularly effective.

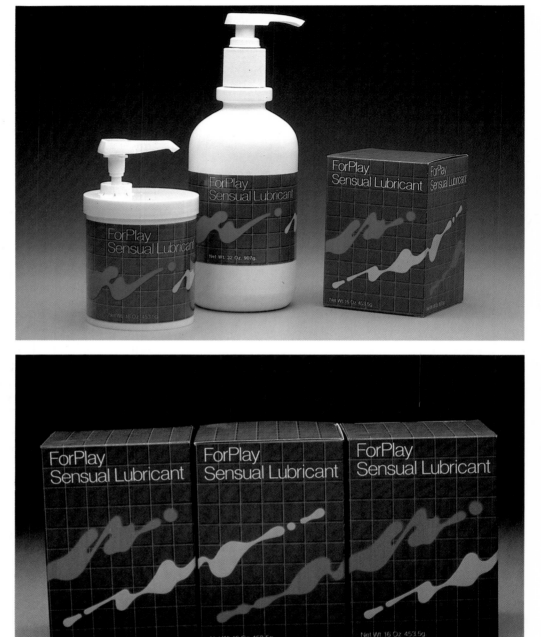

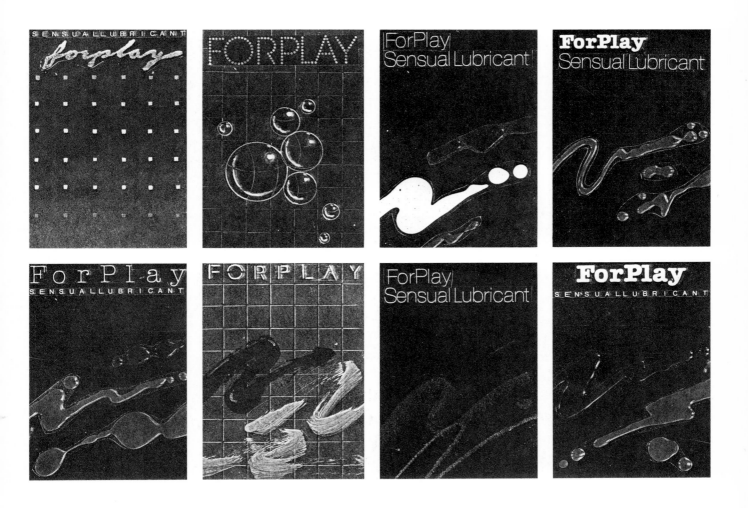

Thumbnail sketches, above, explored a variety of abstract images and techniques. Squares, bubbles, paint strokes and chalk lines were considered along with more obviously biological metaphors.

Client: Trimensa, North Hollywood, CA
Design firm: Bright & Associates, Los Angeles
Designers: Keith Bright, Ray Wood, Peter Sargent, Lynn Berman
Client liaison: Robin Ogilvie
Supplier: Southern California Carton (printer/carton); National Dispenser (production/container)

Perry Ellis Knit
Craft Kit

Martha Voutas Productions was asked to design a package that would sell Perry Ellis designer sweater kits. The idea was to capitalize on this successful designer's reputation for American sportswear with flair. The kits offered the handknit market an opportunity to have a homemade Perry Ellis design.

The package had to accommodate various materials of variable thicknesses from which sweaters could be made for men, women and children in sizes from petite to large. In addition, the package had to hold wools for bulky knits and silks for lightweight vests equally well.

The project involved determining the means of wrapping the yarn. This, ultimately, would determine the design approach. The client emphasized that color and texture were as important as fashion photography to the visual image. Further, the client was adamant that the product should not be packaged in plastic, as he felt that this had

connotations inconsistent with the quality of the kits. A reusable package was also desired.

First, it was decided that winding rather than shanking of yarn was more attractive. Winding, which entails wrapping the yarn around a form, was available at the same cost as shanking, which is simply gathering the yarn in skeins.

Winding was adopted for most designs. However, materials for certain styles, such as camisoles, which are usually made with thin yarns, were shanked because of the relatively small amount involved. Most others were wrapped on cones whose diameter varied according to the density of the nap.

The designers decided that a sleeve was one option for the outside container. A supplier, who produced four-sided sleeves with plastic snap-on caps, was found, but the design was rejected as "too plastic." The designers turned to paper

tube caps. These, when scored, could capture the effect of Perry Ellis's existing corporate graphics. When punched and laced, the caps offered the additional charm of an integral handle for the knitter's cylinder, suggesting reuse as storage. A tag was added so that customers would clearly see and feel the texture of the real yarn, as well as see a photo of the finished garment.

Instructions were designed to be hidden in the bottom of the cap, which was glued on to discourage pilfering. Plastic sleeves were shipped flat-folded and could be cut with standard paper cutters to any length, then drilled for cord threading.

Client: Burren International, New York City
Design firm: Martha Voutas Productions, Inc., New York City
Designers: Adam Hayes, Norico Kanei, Rodney Landi, Allyn Lipari, June Robinson, Martha Voutas
Photographer: Erica Lennard
Suppliers: Neimand Bros (caps); SLM Manufacturing (plastic); Laslo Vartay (plastic); Herlin Press, Inc. (printed tags and instructions); Patterncraft (knitting instructions, fulfillment house, assembly and shipping); Easthouse (packaging consultants)
Client liaisons: Perry Ellis; Laughlin Barker, president; Sydney Brooks, executive vice-president; Nancy Secrist, product manager

Bags, baskets, sleeves, boxes were explored before final design was adopted. Simplicity of solution is apparent in knockdown view, above. Opposite page: Clear, drumlike container is a visual allusion to once popular knitting canister and neatly accommodates hangtag with yarn swatch, far right. Neat crossover is achieved between advertising and packaging programs, above far right.

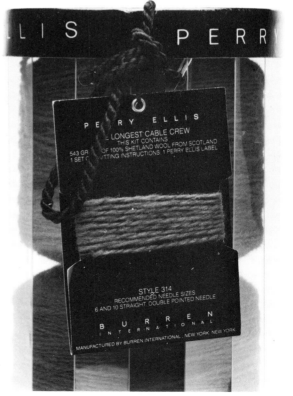

A&W Food Service Redesign

Late in 1981, A&W Food Services of Canada developed a new corporate strategy that involved a massive design effort. The company decided that its packaging, buildings and outdoor illuminated menu boards were seriously in need of a facelift.

A&W retained Samuel Graphic Arts, Inc., to upgrade and enhance the A&W image. The aim was to increase consumer perception of the company's products and packaging and to reposition A&W as a purveyor of quality cooked-to-order food in the fast-food market.

The designers started by establishing and defining formulas that elicit positive consumer attitudes. In redesigning the logo, a consideration was to find a typeface that could easily be hand-lettered for comps. Cooper Black was chosen and, after considerable refinement in testing, became the basis for the packaging solution.

There were several major considerations involved. The company wanted to enlarge its share of market without alienating existing customers. It was also anxious to keep fabrication costs down. Consequently, one of SGA's objectives was to create designs that could be effectively applied to the cartons, pouches, etc., that A&W used.

Working from the old packaging, the designers proceeded from thumbnails to full-scale mockups. Ultimately, 12 alternatives to 10 existing packages were presented to A&W's standards committee. Each of these met A&W's new marketing objectives.

Two of the 12 were selected for group testing. Supergraphic in style, the two were simple and easy to understand. Six color variations were developed for the test marketing.

The final design uses richer and more intense hues of brown and orange, A&W's traditional colors. By changing the emphasis on the colors and using a deep brown for the background and restricting orange to the logotype, the designers felt that consumers would perceive a "down-home" quality. The Cooper Black letters of the logotype with an ampersand holding the letters together made a powerful cartouche on its own, eliminating the need for the A&W oval.

The designers got the inspiration to project the logo on the packages almost as though it was rendered in neon. This approach worked particularly well when applied to the outdoor menu boards, as it was found that projected images work best in all weather conditions.

After 16 months of testing, in which almost 800 designs were comped and tested, the present program was ready to go. The designs have since been extended to store interiors, uniforms, signing and corporate identity.

Old

New

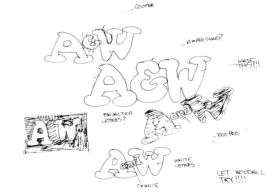

Client: A&W Food Services of Canada
Ltd., North Vancouver, BC
Design firm: Samuel Graphic Arts
Ltd., Vancouver, BC
Designers: Samuel Bowlby, Ron
Woodall, Billy Lee, Mary-Gay Gray, Don
Gallagher, Sharon Williams
Illustrator: Heather Woodall
Photographer: Stanley Wong
Client liaisons: Evan Cardiff, director
of marketing; Paul Hollands, director of
advertising; Ron Davies, purchasing
manager

*Redesign not only included development of
a strong new logotype and typographic
approach, but also involved creating more
powerful photographic product vignettes.
Old product shots, opposite top, were
mundane and lack the taste appeal of the
new, opposite center, which features
luscious images of the fresh ingredients.*

Dynamo

The supermarket remains the most competitive of arenas. Name-brand products jostle one another and their proprietary and no-name competition. Color and graphics leap from the shelves to grab the consumer's attention.

Pricing is also critical. The name of the game is volume and a few pennies per item can make the difference between success or failure. The consumer must be persuaded to spend more. A premium price has to translate into a premium product.

Nowhere is the competition more aggressive than in the household goods aisles, particularly on the detergent shelves. Tried-and-true brands are constantly being challenged even by other lines from their own manufacturer.

Clearly, no one enters this cut-throat sales marathon lightly. Months of analysis and planning lie behind the slightest change, whether in product formulation or packaging appearance. Test marketing acts as the training period before a product goes national. Clearly, everyone is grooming a champion.

In this light, Colgate Palmolive's approach to its Dynamo liquid detergent is instructive. CP had improved the formulation for Dynamo. It wanted a design that would effectively communicate this and be distinctive on the shelf. The aim was to create a bottle and label that would position Dynamo as a winner.

CP put not one but three design firms in its corner. Their professional efforts are responsible for getting the new Dynamo into shape — and providing a new label for that new shape.

The new bottle design creates the impression of maximum size and has a handle for convenience. The shape is muscularly angular to reinforce the powerful nature of the product.

The strong graphic of the label utilizes fluorescent colors to gain attention and direct the consumer's eye to the brand name. The label background color blends with the bright blue bottle to unify the winning package.

Contrast of old and new bottle, below left and right, is particularly startling in light of the fact that both have a 64-oz. capacity. Opposite page: Label treatments explored a number of colorful devices and typographic motifs for maximum shelf impact. Final design, far right below, uses brightly colored chevrons to add to the punch of the intense blue bottle.

Client: Colgate Palmolive, New York City
Design firms: Gregory Fossella Associates (bottle and label design), Boston; Lister/Butler, Inc. (label design), New York City; Tom Carnase Design, Inc. (label design), New York City
Designers: Martin Beck, Gregory Fossella Associates; John Lister, Lister/Butler, Inc.; Tom Carnase
Client liaisons: Barry Seelig, manager/package design; Bonnie Savitz, supervisor/package design

Melitta Coffee Products

Melitta, the leading coffee-making system in Europe, currently competes in the U.S. market in both mass and deluxe retail markets. The current Melitta product line consists of a range of coffee-making equipment and products, including conventional and electric filter drip coffee-makers, accessories, replacement parts, filter papers, and premium coffees.

Some of the Melitta products were sold in identical packages in both grocery and gourmet store outlets, while others were marketed in packages specifically geared to the particular requirements of merchandising conditions. The marketing philosophy of Melitta is directed toward communicating an image of a "system" of coffee-makers, accessories and premium coffees which combine to produce superior flavor.

The assignment for Gerstman + Meyers was to evaluate the current packaging line to determine its strengths and weaknesses. It was felt that by redesigning parts or all of the packaging line, the effectiveness of Melitta packages at point-of-purchase could be greatly improved. G + M strove to create a more strongly integrated family of Melitta packages. While the aim was to more effectively communicate the premium quality of all the products, it was considered equally important to more sharply differentiate between the packages for products sold in grocery stores and those sold through non-food shops. It was felt necessary to more clearly identify each individual product

and to establish a program of cross-referencing within the Melitta "system." The goal was to ensure a level of attractiveness and to maintain design consistency for the entire Melitta packaging line.

The designers retained the well-known orange and green color scheme for the grocery line and used warmly hued photographs for the deluxe products sold through gourmet outlets. Overall brand identification was maintained through the use of an orange band with the Melitta logo on all packages. This solution eliminated numerous graphic inconsistencies. It provided a stronger identification across the Melitta line.

New packaging with its strong family associations is featured as part of print and TV advertising, opposite below.

Client: Melitta, Inc., Cherry Hill, NJ
Design firm: Gerstman+Meyers, Inc., New York City
Designers: Herbert M. Meyers; Juan Concepcion, vice-president, group design director; Larry Riddell, vice-president, design director; Jon Lopez, account manager.
Photographer: David Pruitt
Illustrators: Julia Noonan, Sal Santelli, Barney Plotkin, Elias Marge
Suppliers: Diamond Paper Box (deluxe coffee maker and coffee warmer packages), Simkins Industries (coffee filter packages), Crown Cork & Seal (coffee packages), Medina Studios (retouching)

Ralston Purina
Butcher's Blend

When Ralston Purina introduced Butcher's Blend, the idea was to appeal to the palate of the people who were concerned with their dogs' nutrition. Unfortunately, this approach was less than successful. Initial sales fell below reasonable expectations.

Ralston Purina considered the problem and concluded that the package failed to capitalize on the product's meaty flavor. There were other areas of difficulty as well, notably the effectiveness of the product's facing. Frequently, pet foods are stacked so that only the bottom areas of the package may be read from the aisle.

On the new package, created by Lister Butler, the redesigned and enlarged logo leaps out at customers. The bright red background further ensures attention on the shelf.

Red was chosen for its raw meat imagery, an image enhanced by a photograph showing the product spread on a butcher's block.

Sales registered an increase almost immediately. Within six months of the introduction of the new package, Butcher's Blend gained 20 per cent more market. This success can be traced to a print and TV advertising campaign that prominently featured the new package.

Client: Ralston Purina, St. Louis
Design firm: Lister Butler, Inc., New York City
Designers: John Lister, design director; Anita K. Hersh, Dennis Brubaker, designers
Photographer: Ron DeMilt
Client liaisons: Andy Bresler, group product manager; Stuart Maugen, product manager; Lisa Cast, assistant product manager

Butcher's Blend

NOW MORE MEATY TASTE · 100% COMPLETE & BALANCED

Dog Food

Brand ®

·Beef, Bacon & Liver Flavor·

Net Wt. 4.5 lbs. (2.04 kg)

Purina ®

Butcher's Blend

NOW MORE MEATY TASTE · 100% COMPLETE & BALANCED

Dog Food

Brand ®

Cobraline Auto Ignition Parts

Cobraline Manufacturing Company had a new brand of automotive replacement parts with a modern, high-tech look. Cobraline had decided that the packaging would be the major component for introducing this line and retained designer Sandra Meyers. The packaging program would have to include hangcards and boxes. There were hundreds of part numbers.

The products were directed to the "do-it-yourselfer." They would be found in a self-service retail environment rather than at a professional automotive parts distributor. The packaging system had to provide customer assistance in the absence of a sales clerk. It also had to be able to accommodate additions to the line. The client wanted to keep the number of boxes to a minimum for economy and inventory control. Further, this limit in boxes would also assist the retailer.

The consumer's confidence in his ability to install the part by himself had to be encouraged. This could be enhanced by easy identification of parts and simplified instructions and installation diagrams.

A high-tech appeal was conveyed through the simplicity of the packaging and its design components. Each package has a background grid. In some cases, the package carries a stylized illustration of the part. In the case of blister cards, the part itself is displayed against the grid. Typography identifies the name of the part and the make of the car that the part fits.

All packaging is color-coded according to car make so as to acclimate the customer easily and direct him to the right section within the automotive department. Vehicle application data and installation instructions on the back panel were designed to highlight pertinent information.

The package also had to look clean, but not fancy. This meant not using photography, especially four-color photography.

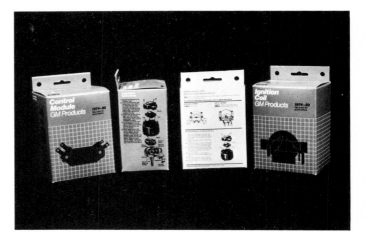

Client: Cobraline Manufacturing Corp., Westbury, NY
Design firm: Sandra Meyers, New York City
Designers: Frank Ziella, Sandra Meyers
Illustrator: Sandra Meyers
Client liaisons: Joseph Shekel, president; Les Green, vice-president/marketing; Joseph DeStephano, vice-president/manufacturing

Kaopectate

The Upjohn Company retained Fredrick Z. Vallarta Associates to revitalize its Kaopectate product line. The problem was that, while the company's regular formula was the leading product in the category, the visuals were felt to be weak, dated, and lacking impact at point-of-purchase. At the same time, the concentrated line of the product was also not producing the expected sales. A significant part of the assignment was to develop package graphics that would lend greater impact and more appeal to both the regular and concentrated formulas without the one undercutting the other.

FZV developed a logotype which projected a strong, authoritative image. These qualities were obtained through the use of a bold, condensed typeface, chosen for maximum impact and legibility on the package facing. Italics were used to suggest the fast-working nature of the product.

Gray was maintained as the color for the label of the regular formula to ensure continuity. However, the tone was deepened to enhance the contrast with the white bottle and to achieve a fresher, more contemporary image.

The same approach was taken for the concentrate. The pink color was maintained, but deepened, with three horizontal bands added to achieve instant attention. This, it was felt, communicates a better tasting, more flavorful product.

Sales have increased for both regular and concentrate since the redesign was introduced, a fact the client attributes to the new packaging.

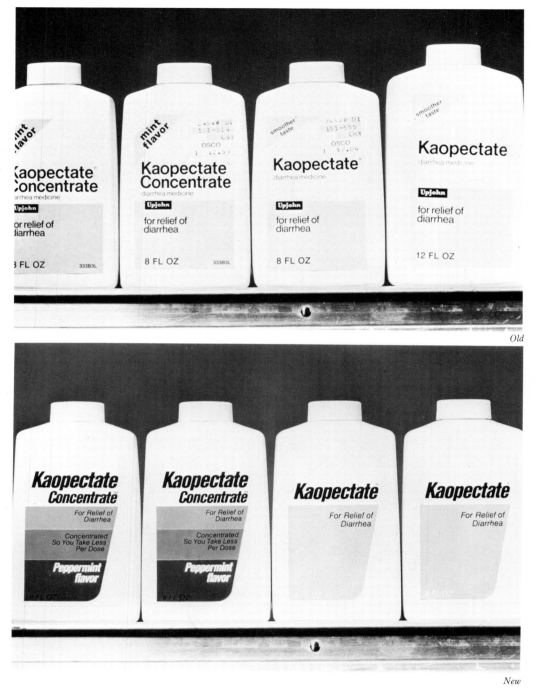

Old

New

Number one with pharmacists for the ninth straight year.

Kaopectate Concentrate is preferred by many families because of its peppermint flavor and smaller dosage.

For generations Kaopectate has been the most often recommended diarrhea remedy.

Ask your Upjohn representative for special winter/flu season allowances.

©1982 The Upjohn Company

"I drank the water! I know I'll need The Specialist."

Unfamiliar water or food can cause diarrhea. And nothing spoils a vacation or a good time faster. So take along The Specialist. Kaopectate. It it's the only leading non-prescription medicine created just for diarrhea. It contains natural active ingredients. And Kaopectate is so effective it relieves your diarrhea within 24 hours. After all, you've waited too long for a vacation to have it spoiled by diarrhea.

Kaopectate. The Specialist.

New package, opposite below, provides stronger brand identity and a more powerful shelf image than the old, above. New label treatment grew out of early examinations of abstract forms and combinations of bands, far left. Final design has become an important part of the client's print and TV advertising.

Client: The Upjohn Co., Kalamazoo, MI
Design firm: Frederick Z. Vallarta & Associates, Inc., Chicago
Designers: Jack Kellbach, design director; Sam Ciulla, Leslie Mangas, designers
Client liaisons: Jim Stevenson; Warren Smith, product manager; Walter Ruemer, design director

Bumble Bee
Limited Catch

The problem for Michael Mabry Design was to create a label for a new premium albacore product. The product was to sell itself but the package had to be tasteful and reserved in style. It was necessary to use the Bumble Bee trademark and "Bee" on the label as well as such mandated information as the UPC code, weight, and nutritional data.

Within the small amount of space permitted on a seven-ounce can, the objective was to create a look to surpass that of any other tuna product on the shelf. At the same time, the label had to have a double-faced panel, similar to that for the existing solid white albacore produced by Bumble Bee Seafoods.

The designers developed a trademark, "Limited Catch," that became the focal point of the label. The color scheme, which contained references to the label for solid white albacore, also visually stressed the product difference. The background color was changed to cream and MMD used burgundy foil for the striping on the top and bottom. The designers felt this gave the product the proper feeling of quality and exclusivity, without losing the advantages of brand loyalty inherent under the Bumble Bee umbrella.

Limited Catch, produced in small quantities, is designed to sell itself without the assistance of any promotion or advertising. A point-of-purchase display unit, featuring the same burgundy, cream and gold Limited Catch trademark, was produced with a header describing the special quality of the product.

Client: Bumble Bee Seafoods, Castle & Cooke, Inc., San Diego, CA
Design firm: Michael Mabry Design, San Francisco
Designers: Michael Mabry, art director/designer; Margie Eng-Chu, assistant designer
Illustrator: Tim Girvin
Client liaisons: Bruce Martin, vice-president, marketing and sales; Arie Noot, product manager, U.S.A.

Ekco Bakeware

John Racila Associates had to develop a product strategy for a new line of commercial quality baking pans to be sold by Ekco. Ekco wanted to project the pan's professional quality with brand name, logotype and label design. The idea was to suggest the transition from the restaurant to the home kitchen.

The designers explored several brand-name options. The choice was crucial, as it would establish the product's position in the marketplace. JRA developed a series of ciphers for the logotype. These were tested for compatibility with the product concept and the product itself. JRA then developed support graphics to establish the product's appeal in department stores and gourmet shops.

The name "Great Reflections" was selected to reinforce the effectiveness of a shiny metal surface for achieving professional baking results. All visual elements of the logotype and support graphics are controlled to evoke the precise measurement associated with professional cookery. Black-and-white graphics extend this image and provide a dramatic visual foil for the word "Great" printed in red. "Great" is treated almost casually and this serves to emphasize it even more. The word is part of the brand name, yet its distinctive treatment is both a claim and a promise.

Client: Ekco Housewares Co., Franklin Park, IL
Design firm: John Racila Associates, Oak Brook, IL
Designers: John Racila, coordinator/creative director; John Neher, design director; John Metz, John Neher, Laura Garza, designers
Client liaisons: Elliot Black, vice-president/marketing; Judy Cline, group product manager; Bob Balow, product manager

Pan labels convey a slick, professional image at point-of-purchase and are particularly appropriate to the line.

72000

great!
REFLECTIONS.
BY EKCO.

PIE PAN · 9" x 1¼"
Great Reflections Bakeware is made of 100% first quality stainless steel. Its durable finish is resistant to wear, won't corrode or tarnish and polishes to a brilliant luster. With normal use stainless steel will not chip, dent or scratch. Simple soap and water clean-up insures many years of dependable service. Prompt drying will prevent water spots. Stainless steel is also dishwasher safe.
© 1982 EKCO Housewares Co., Franklin Park, IL 60131 · Made and Printed in Korea

Polaroid Cameras

Polaroid's design department had to create new packaging for the four consumer cameras sold by the company. The aim was to use a value-oriented approach to disabuse consumers of any negative attitudes regarding the status of Polaroid cameras. Existing packaging featured childlike, circus graphics which seemed to say "toy" rather than "equipment."

The solution was to concentrate on the product. The designers recommended that the camera be shown photographically. They had the idea to project the product on the package in a three-dimensional manner. Each facing had a different view: front and back, left and right. Black was suggested for the background to impart elegance.

Against this background, the product acquires the high-tech character of expensive, precision equipment. The packages have a visual affinity to those for other luxurious products, such as fine china.

Traditional boxboard printed in five colors was used, along with special UV liquid laminate coatings. These reduced the incidence of tell-tale fingerprints. The coatings also made the boxes less susceptible to slipping off one another when stacked.

Package photography presents the product in a holographic form to convey the sophisticated character of the equipment.

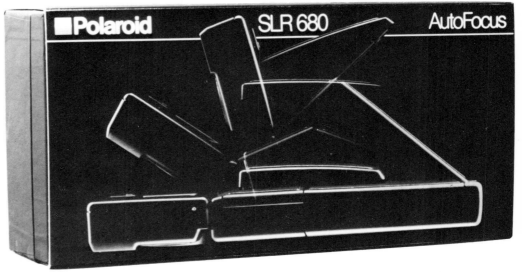

Client: Polaroid, Cambridge, MA
Design firm: Polaroid Design Dept.
Designers: Michael Benes, Bill Tomlinson, Carol Olsen, Jim Fesler, Ted Holloran
Supplier: Acme Printing
Photographer: Steve Grohe Photography

Westin Hotels
Gift Package

The assignment for John Hornall Design Works was to design the package for a series of gift items that was being developed as an extension of the new Westin Hotels corporate identity program. While guests at Westin hotels are accustomed to special touches in their hotel rooms, this gift package was to have a unique quality.

Items for the package were collected from different suppliers all over the world. There was a need, therefore, to develop an outside container that maintained consistency and quality.

John Hornall Design Works ran a computer search to locate the top folding carton manufacturer. A designer from the office then visited nine plants. The idea was to determine what manufacturing techniques would result in the best-looking end product. Consideration was given to

such things as on-line lacquer vs. off-line lacquer, friction lock vs. slit-lock flaps, etc. Finally, the choice had to be made of which plant was best able to guarantee the necessary level of quality. Arkay Packaging was the supplier ultimately selected.

To aid Westin hotels in maintaining proper inventories, the supplier sub-contracted a packager to load the filled boxes and distribute them directly to the 55 hotels in the Westin chain. To test potential color schemes, designers produced prototypes of the six core items. A dark reflective gray was selected for its neutrality and its elegant look. Tests proved that the dark gray would reflect and harmonize with the variety of guest room color schemes found in the hotels throughout the world.

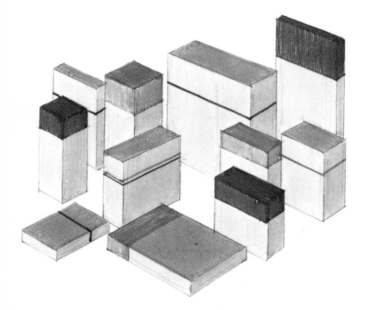

Old packaging, opposite top, had a ho-
hum, impersonal character. Various
alternatives were explored, using different
motifs and type styles. Nesting of all
same-size packaging, opposite bottom, was
considered. The vocabulary of rules and
bars associated with more expensive
cosmetic products was examined, using
rules of different widths.
Final design features blind-embossed
symbol, embossed foil rule and foil-
stamped type.

Client: Westin Hotels, Seattle
Design firm: John Hornall Design Works, Seattle
Designers: Jack R. Anderson, John Hornall
Supplier: Arkay Packaging Corp.
Client liaison: Ron LaRue, director of marketing